Credit Repair Secrets:

Increase Your Credits Score in 30
Days with Secret Technique.
609 Letters Templates
Included.
Repair Your Negative Profile
Fast!
And Develop Millionaire
Mindset
with Great Score!

*Disclaimer: No Financial Gains
Guaranteed Whatsoever

Table of Contents

Introduction

If there ever was a change that has affected us quite greatly in the age of the Internet, it would have been our increasing dependence on data. It is as seems that every interaction we have made in this day and age could not have been made possible without an exchange of information, whether willingly or not.

This is all the more prevalent in several industries and systems wherein institutions can approve or reject any application without having to so much as to personally interact with the person. All they have to do is to look at your information and determine for themselves whether or not you are worth the risk investing on.

And this is where our credit scores come into play. Prepared by different agencies and used heavily by banks and other organizations as references, our credit scores can dictate what options we can avail of as far as several financial products, services, and even job opportunities are concerned.

Do you want to apply for a loan? The lender will look at your credit report. You want to rent an apartment unit or purchase a parcel of land on an installment basis? The landlord and realtor will look at your credit report. You want to apply for a job handling money or private information? The employer will look at your credit report.

As such, having a good credit score means that you won't have a lot of impediments when you apply for something. On the other hand, a poor one can set you back in several ways.

Just keep in mind that the score is just comprised of two digits and nothing more. However, the weight that such numbers carry should not be underestimated. Depending on what score you are given, the chances of you being approved or rejected for an important application will be considerable.

Conventionally, building your credit score will take quite a while and will require you to perform several noteworthy credit-based actions. But how you are supposed to build on your score when your current score prevents you from getting into several good opportunities for credit-building? On the surface, it could seem like getting a bad credit score starts a self-defeating cycle where you are unable to do something to improve your score which, in turn, lowers your credit score even more.

Believe it or not, it is quite possible to build on your credit score. You don't even have to do something creative or even out of the ordinary to get your score out of the danger zone. Better yet, you don't have to wait long to see improvements in your score.

In this book, "Credit Repair Secrets: Increase Your Credits Score in 30 Days with Secret Technique", I propose the theory that you can build on your credit score and make it reach acceptable levels in just a month and with little to no cost on your part.

Basing on my own experience in the financial market as well as from my personal life, I have laid out a roadmap for which you can build on your credit score and get to wherever you want without being impeded by what your credit report is saying to you.

To do that, you must first understand the exact nature of a credit score. What is it and why has it become quite an important figure nowadays? In this book, you will learn how credit reports are being used currently and what comprises them.

Then, you will learn how your credit scores can change from one period to another. You might be surprised by what actions you usually make (or refrain from making) that will affect your score. Yes, even the acts that you think were innocent and inconsequential will contribute to that score you get periodically.

Once you have learned all that you can about what makes up your score and how it can be changed, we can then go about building on it. It does not matter if you have a relatively young credit life or have one for quite a while. There is always a way to build on your score that is legit and inexpensive.

One crucial lesson you will also learn here is the qualities needed to have a good credit score. Your character and the habits that you form will contribute to what reporting agencies are saying about you. As such, you must be open to the idea of making some important lifestyle changes here and there to improve on your score.

And what if your score happens to be so low? Is there a way to build on it and still get a hold of important loans and services? The answer is yes. You only have to know what to look for and where. Fortunately, I have also laid out a few options that you can avail of to get a hold of important funds while you are still fixing or building your score.

Of course, you will also learn what NOT to do to improve on your score. You might be surprised at the number of pitfalls you can easily find yourself with your credit activities if you are not careful. As such, learning what these pitfalls and mistakes are is crucial to avoid finding yourself in a predicament.

And lastly, you will learn how to build on your success and keep the momentum going. I will not only teach you how to build on your credit score so that it turns from poor to acceptable. I will also lay out a few strategies that will turn an acceptable score into an excellent one.

The point that I am trying to get on is that credit building and credit repair need not be expensive, complicated, or protracted. You can get yours to a level acceptable to a lot of lenders in just a few weeks and some well-made financial decisions here and there.

And if you are ready to learn what it takes to improve on your score, turn the page and start reading.

Have fun!

Chapter I: The Basics of Your Credit Score

Before anything else, you should understand how much of an impact your credit score leaves on your life. to do this, you must first know how they work.

What is a Credit Score?

The simplest definition of a credit score is that it is the final mark that a credit reporting agency gives to you for every quarter or period. Think of it as a grade that a teacher gives to their students every quarter but with a wider range of application.

Credit scores are designed to make it easier for lenders, employers, and other people to make a decision when transacting with you.

The premise is simple: that credit report is highly detailed but going through all of that takes a bit of time.

For a bank that deals with hundreds of people at any given instance, they need some point of reference that helps them decide within seconds. And this is where a credit score comes into play.

So, what are lenders looking at you specifically? They are trying to find out the degree of risk they will subject themselves when they do business with you. In essence, a credit score will tell them if you are worth the investment or not.

To understand this better, here is a scenario. Let us say that two people are applying for the same type of loan in a certain bank. Person A has a credit score of 600 from FICO. Person B has a FICO score of 400.

Regardless of their circumstances, it is most likely that Person A will have his application approved than Person B. All that the bank agent had to do was to look at their score and come up with a decision in seconds.

And, mind you, Person A's score is not even that impressive as 600 is rather average. It is just that his score will allow him a slightly higher percentage of getting his application approved compared to the person with a lower score.

Do Lenders Always Refer to Credit Scores?

Are banks and employers mandated to always look at credit reports and scores before making a decision? No.

Your credit score, by design, is meant to serve as a reference for businesses before they approve or reject your application. What that implies is that a credit score, though a reliable source, is not the only element that a business has to factor in when they approve or reject your application.

There are instances when people with poor credit scores can get a hold of loans with manageable payment rates. This usually happens if the lender knows the applicant personally or has been doing business with them in the past.

However, they are the exception to the rule. Generally speaking, a bank will look at your credit score before they approve or reject your application especially if you are a total stranger to them.

The Importance of a Good Score

What you have to understand now is that a credit score can dictate what financial products you can avail of and what transactions you can take part in. A good credit score can open to you several benefits and opportunities which will include the following.

A. Better Approval Rates

The first and most direct benefit of a good score is that it will increase your chances of being approved for a new line of credit. A lot of lenders would just look at your score and come up with a decision on whether or not to approve your application.

However, what you must realize is that a good score is not a guarantee for instant approval. It merely increases your chances of getting approved. A lender will still have to look at outside factors to determine whether or not you are worth the risk.

A good credit score, however, is mostly enough to tell any lender that you have what it takes to comply with any financial obligation that you have signed yourself up for.

B. Interest Rates

The interest rate is the lender's way of making money from their investment in you. After all, they'd want that money to grow. What's the point of lending you that money if it does not grow while your contract still exists?

And, more often than not, your interest rate can be affected by your credit score. A good credit score would increase your chances of having to deal with a more manageable interest rate while a poor score will result in the maximum possible interest rates.

Think of interest as the lender's "security" to ensure that you pay your dues in time. The bigger it is, the more motivated you will be to get that obligation off of your record.

However, if you have to deal with a lower interest rate, you can also save up more money to pay the entire debt off quickly. In other words, a credit score will ultimately help you settle your debts quickly by way of your interest rate.

C. High Credit Limits

Aside from the interest, the amount that you can borrow tends to increase with your credit score. The reason for this is that your credit score will indicate to the bank or lender that you have what it takes to pay off every debt that you willingly signed yourself up for.

In short, a credit score that is above average will give the impression to a lender that you are trustworthy enough to be loaned a sizeable amount. With a low score, you would still have a chance to get your application approved but the amount might be more limited in size.

D. Better Negotiating Power

Your credit score can be used as leverage whenever you apply for a loan. For instance, suppose that a lender offers you this amount and for a certain interest rate. The problem is that you don't find their offer to be appealing.

If this were to happen, you can use your good credit score to tell that lender that you have received other offers from other lenders which are more favorable to you. Sure, what you are doing is technically bluffing but there is a chance that the lender will cave in and give you a more manageable rate.

With a decent to bad credit score, however, you are never in a position to bargain for your payment terms. What you get is literally what is being offered at the table. Nothing else.

E. Easier Rental

One of the more recently added benefits with credit scores is the ability to get quickly approved when you rent a room or an apartment unit. This because landlords now use a system to screen out all applicants based on their credit scores.

So, does a bad credit score mean that you will get instantly rejected by a landlord? The answer is no. What landlords are looking for are bad scores that are caused by rent-related issues. Perhaps you were kicked out of your previous apartment because you were a lousy tenant. Or perhaps you were behind several months in your rental fees.

What this also means is that landlords can now report you to the different reporting agencies for any outstanding or delinquent balance you have with them. This, in turn, will be reflected in your credit scores which will warn other landlords to refrain from doing business with you.

F. Other Benefits

The benefits above are some of the more general benefits that you can enjoy from a good credit score. However, there are some other benefits that you can take advantage of depending on the region you live in and the businesses you interact with.

For instance, car insurance companies can offer those with good credit scores with fewer penalties and better coverage. In essence, you get to avail yourself of a wider-applying insurance plan with premiums that are more manageable on your part.

Another lesser-known benefit is offered by cell phone service providers who would offer those with good credit scores better deals for their plans. Some providers even remove the need for a security deposit and the ability to purchase the most recent phone models at a discounted price.

Lastly, some utility companies offer those with good credit scores more manageable fees if they have to relocate. This means the probability that you don't have to deal with a security deposit or generally lower fees for the first few months on wherever you are going to move into.

The point is that other sectors in the community are finding ways to provide incentives so that people with good credit scores will avail themselves of their products and services. This only means that you are better off having a good credit score for reasons that go beyond mere loaning.

The Downsides of a Decent to Poor Credit Score

So, what happens if your credit score is not as good as you want it to be? As was stated before, your credit score can influence a lot of aspects of your financial life. For poor credit score holders, the disadvantages can be summarized in three categories which are:

l Lower approval chances.
l Less manageable loan terms and interest rates.
l Limit credit choices and other related options.

When you have a bad credit score, you will find out that bankers are more apprehensive with your applications. Sure, some lenders might approve of your loan but most will avoid you like the plague. Again, this goes back to your score giving them a poor impression of your ability to manage your financial obligations.

And even if you do get your loan approved, you will be set with harsher and more difficult payment terms. This is the lender's only way of ensuring that you do pay up your obligation and mitigate some of the risks that they will be exposed to for doing business with you.

These payment terms usually come in the form of high interest or high annual fees. Either way, you will end up paying more than the amount you initially loaned if you have a bad credit score.

And lastly, you will have limited options when it comes to credit lines. This can be problematic as opening new credit lines is one of the strategies that you can employ to build on your credit score.

So how are you supposed to build on your credit score if you are not legally allowed to avail of the many options to build on the same? Granted, there will be some options for you still but they are not mainstream. And you will get to know them a few chapters from here.

To Summarize

In essence, your credit score can influence a lot of the transactions that you are bound to make. This does not only involve loaning money but even finding a job, a place to live in, and even services to be subscribed to.

The point is that a good credit score is going to be beneficial for you in the long term. Sure, there are other elements to consider before lenders and business approve your application but your credit score will tell them one thing and one thing only:

You have what it takes to deal with your debts in the most efficient and trustworthy manner possible.

But what exactly are lenders looking for to allow you to enjoy some of the benefits that they offer. It is not enough that you have a good credit score. You must have an excellent one.

Chapter II: Your Credit Score

Now that you know what impact your credit score brings to your life, the next question to ask is this:

How is it calculated?

Your credit score is just comprised of three digits but how it can influence your transactions in the future should not be underestimated. So you have to wonder how did the reporting agencies even come up with your score every quarter.

The process is rather simple but you must acquaint yourself with how your score is being prepared.

What Comprises Your Score?

First and foremost, you have to understand that your credit score is being prepared under one system: FICO. Made by the Fair Isaac Corporation, the FICO scoring system measures your trustworthiness as a credit holder on a range from 300 to 850.

The figures are directly proportional to your creditworthiness. The higher the score, the most likely you are going to enjoy the benefits laid out just a chapter ago.

So, how is your score going to be calculated under the FICO system? The company has yet to divulge their calculation formula but is quite known that they always looked at five components. In turn, these components comprise a considerable portion of your score. They are as follows.

A. Payment History

Contribution to your Score: 35%

This component takes into account your overall activity as a credit holder. As the name would imply, this component records every payment you have made and missed for every credit or service you have subscribed to.

This component would also factor in every collection that was made on you, every bankruptcy you have declared, and your delinquencies. What is crucial in this component is not only the size of the payments you have made but also the time it took for you to settle all your accounts.

The general rule with your Payment History is that the more outstanding issues you have, the lower your score under this component would be.

B. Amount Owed

Contribution to your Score: 30%

The second-largest contributor to your score, the amount that you ow indicate your level of risk to a lender by way of the credit you use on any given period. Credit utilization simply pertains to the amount of credit that you use up with the limit that you are given.

Aside from the amount of credit that you use, this component also records the amount of debt that you currently have. This will account for the different accounts that you have opened and their type.

For this component, the general rule is that your rate is inversely proportional to your level of risk. The more credit you move, the riskier you are. As such, a lot of lenders would look at this portion to see if you have what it takes to abide by their terms if they approve your loan.

C. Credit History

Contribution to your Score: 15%

This component simply records the length of your activity as a credit holder. As such, it will benefit you greatly if you can hold and maintain certain lines of credit without getting them delinquent even once.

For example, if you are a credit holder that has never missed a payment on an account for 20 years, that consistency will be required here to your favor.

Of course, those who are new to the act of maintaining credit cannot rely on this component in their early years.

However, there's a caveat under this component: if you close a long-standing account, you will negatively impact your score. The reason for this is that you effectively removed entire years of transactions from your history.

D. New Credit

Whenever you open a new line of credit, it will serve as a demerit under this category. The reason for this is that most lenders would see you opening a new credit line as you need money.

One other reason is that every new credit line would necessitate a hard search on your financial information. This means that the lender would go out of their way to draw your financial information from the reporting agencies.

A hard search does not exactly damage your credit score but multiple ones that were done within short periods from each other would. This is a tell-tale sign that the credit holder is becoming desperate for money and might not be able to handle the obligations that would be imposed on them.

As such, every new line of credit you open will damage your score under this category. Do it often in a short period and your credit score will go down considerably in the next report you get.

E. Credit Mix

Contribution to your Score: 10%

Under this component, the agencies would look into the diversity of credit that you are maintaining. A healthy credit mix is a strong indicator that you have what it takes to handle all your debts which makes you less risky for a potential lender.

There are two types of credit being included here. The first is Revolving Credit which would include your credit cards, loyalty cards from a retail business, and other lines of credit.

The second class is what is called Installment Credit. This will include any mortgages you have as well as your loans.

To make things easier for you, here's a visual representation of the composition of your FICO Credit Score:

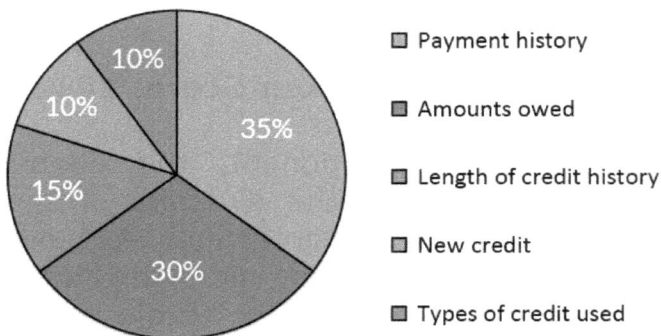

- Payment history
- Amounts owed
- Length of credit history
- New credit
- Types of credit used

So, What's not Included?

At a glance, you could tell that your credit score is going to be derived from purely financial and transactional information. In short, any action you make that involves the use, transfer, and acquiring of money and credit will be included here.

As such, character-based and personal information will not be included here. After all, lenders could care less about your race, gender, and employment type. What they are most particular about is your ability to manage your debts which the components above are more likely to indicate.

But, surprisingly enough, there will be other financial information that would not be generally included. This includes the length of employment you have, your annual income, and even your rental payments. As to why they are excluded is only something that FICO knows for now.

However, there are services out there that can help you make your other financial information stand out more in your credit score. And you will get to know them later.

Score Range

FICOs score range is not exactly universally applied. Every credit reporting agency has even their way of treating your financial information and categorizing every score.

However, just keep in mind that the agencies do not offer widely varying interpretations of your credit information. If you have a decent score in Experian, your score in TransUnion will likely be largely the same with some minor differences here and there.

The point is that the agencies will use the same structure for coming up with your score and will use the same range which is as follows:

Range	Grade
300 to 579	Poor
580 to 669	Decent
670 to 379	Good
740 to 799	Very Good
800 and beyond	Excellent

A. Poor

Under this range, you are considered by most lenders that you are a risky person to lend money to. Most lenders would avoid doing business with you. However, there are some programs available that might help you get funding while also letting you improve your credit score.

B. Decent

A score under this range means that you might not be as risky as the previous class but you are still a considerably risky credit holder. Generally, this is the baseline for credit holders in the sense that they start here.

Alternatively, if you have been an active credit holder and had made a few mistakes, you are most likely to end here.

Either way, you can use this range as a good start for your credit building and repair strategy. A lot of lenient lenders will approve loans of people with scores under this range but they will still impose heavy payment terms and interest rates.

C. Good

For you, this should be the standard to start aiming for because this is where things get manageable on your part. Under this range, you can get approved for a loan with a more favorable payment term.

In some cases, you can even use this score to boost your chances of getting better insurance premiums and get employed in some jobs.

D. Very Good

At this range, lenders will consider you to be a very reliable borrower. As such, they will relax their terms while allowing you to loan more than what you previously ask for.

At this range, you can also avail of more favorable interest rates, premiums, and payment terms for financial products, services, and other forms of subscriptions.

E. Excellent

This is the final range and is considered by lenders to be the highest standard any credit holder can achieve. At this range, you are considered a safe investment for lenders. Some might even find you to be so safe that they can allow you a sizeable loan with the most favorable payment terms for you.

At this range, you can even enjoy all of the benefits offered by non-finance subscriptions and other services. When you reach this range, there is nothing else to do but to keep your score at a high for as long as possible.

The Reporting Agencies

Aside from knowing how your credit report is being repaired, you also need to know who prepares them. As of now, three major reporting agencies are operating in various regions across the world. They are:

A. Equifax

Having been servicing the public since 1899, you could say that Equifax is one of the first and oldest credit reporting agencies out there. And aside from reporting your credit activities, Equifax is also in the business of protecting you from consumer fraud as well as identity theft.

For their century-long existence, Equifax had only one blemish in 2017 and it involves a data breach where the information of millions of subscribers was comprised by hackers. Fortunately, Equifax has since fixed that breach and is offering more services that allow you to monitor your credit information for free.

B. Experian

This CRA traces its origins back to London in the 1800s. a century later, Experian operates in 39 territories across the world and employs more than 17,000 agents.

The company also offers other services aside from credit reporting. They offer credit holders tools to which they could monitor their credit data as well as assistance in amending erroneous or missing entries.

As of the late 2010s, Experian uses the FICO 8 system which means that their treatment of your financial data is slightly different but more accurate to FICO's most recent algorithm. Whether or not that ends in an accurate credit score is something that you would have to decide for yourself if you subscribe to their services.

C. TransUnion

Starting as a holding company for tank cars in the 1960s, TransUnion made the shift to credit reporting by the 1980s and has remained in that industry ever since. Today, TransUnion is one of the 3 major CRAs that operate in 30 countries and serves more than 1 billion people.

Aside from credit reporting, TransUnion can also help in protecting your data from fraud and theft. It also offers monitoring services for your financial data and maintains an open line of communication with the other two CRAs.

Why are there 3 Major CRAs?

Have you ever wondered why there are three separate credit reporting agencies even if they use the same formula and method? There are three answers to this. The first and most obvious one is that they can. There is no law stating that there should only be one CRA in every region.

There is no limit as to how many CRAs should operate in the world. It is only just that TransUnion, Equifax, and

Experian were the only ones that managed to sustain their operations.

The second reason is that each CRA offers a different perspective on your credit information. They have slight variations in how they treat data. For instance, Experian might look more into the amount that you owe and have paid while TransUnion would look at your credit mix and credit history.

The point is that these CRAs can give reports that may differ from each other slightly but would support the other. If you are wondering why you got such a score in Experian, you can look at TransUnion for a more detailed explanation on why you got such a rating.

So, do credit reporting agencies talk to each other? The answer is technically no. There are policies and laws set in place that prevents companies from sharing the information that they gather from you to protect your privacy.

The only exception here is in the instance that you become a victim of fraud and identity theft. If such were to happen, the agencies can share information and with authorities to prevent further crimes from being committed with your data.

The third reason is choice. You should understand that not all creditors report to all 3 reporting agencies. At best, they would report to one or two of the CRAs. This explains why you would get different scores from the three agencies.

This also means that lenders could refer to one or two CRA reports when deciding on your application. This is because pulling all three reports can be expensive on their part.

The Reporting Process

How your reports are prepared is a process that is quite simple and straightforward. It only involves two steps.

The first step is collecting all your data. A CRA would receive reports from lenders and businesses regarding your activities. This means every payment you made, the balance you have cleared, accounts that were marked as delinquent, and every remark about the way you handle your finances will be reported to the agency.

Aside from this, the agency might also look into public records about you. Court cases where you were declared as bankrupt or insolvent to even changes in your address or registry in the local list of voters would also be looked into in this phase.

Once every relevant information has been gathered, the reporting agency would then start the painstaking labor of interpreting your data and using FICO's calculating system to come up with your credit report and score. All the data that they have gathered will be summarized in your report to support the score that they gave to you.

Using Your Report

What happens with your report once it is made, then? The CRA will keep a copy of that document for your reference in case you request your information. They could also send it to you regularly as part of their service.

You can also request a copy of your credit report from time to time. Perhaps you want to apply for a loan and would want to spare the lender the effort of having to pull up your file from the CRAs.

If this were the case, you should know that you are entitled to one free copy of your credit report for every reporting period. The second one you will request will come with a fee. After all, the agency has to pay the people that would collect your data and compute your score.

Also, the CRA can "sell" the information contained therein to companies. However, there's a catch. Under consumer protection and privacy laws, the CRAs cannot give such information to just about anyone asking for your data. That entity has to have a valid legal ground as to why they should be given a copy of your report.

For instance, a lender would want to make sure that they could trust you with their money. To do this, they would want to take a look at your credit history. As such, they have a valid legal ground for which to ask any of the three CRAs of your financial information.

Are Credit Reports Final and

Irrevocable?

The short answer to this question is NO. FICO's system might be purely mathematical and the process mechanical but your report is still going to be prepared by actual human beings. That means that your report is just as infallible as the agents making it.

If you feel that your credit report is erroneous, you can always dispute it at the agency that prepared it. If they feel that their report is correct, they will give you a detailed explanation as to how they came up with your score.

But if there truly was an error in your data, then the company is compelled to make amendments. You will then receive an amended credit report within a week or so after the dispute is settled.

What this simply means is that you have to scrutinize your credit report when it is sent to you. Is all the data correct? Are there any missing payments? Did the agency incorrectly interpret one activity of yours?

You have to know how your data is being treated by the agencies. For all you know, you might have a score that could be at the above-average to excellent ranges if all that data was present and properly interpreted by the CRAs. A few amendments later and you could have a score that truly reflects your trustworthiness as a credit holder.

However, just keep in mind that such incidents are more of an exception than the norm. For the rest of the book, we would assume that the CRA is correct and you indeed deserve your poor credit rating.

Chapter III: Why Credit Scores Go Bad

As was stated a few chapters ago, the benefits of having a good credit score are not to be underestimated. If you get yours at the very good to excellent ranges, you can practically coast through your life with good deals on loans, insurances, other financial products, and even tangible services. You might even get a good freebie or three along the way.

The point is that you, as a credit holder, will be better off having a good rating. But what happens if your score sinks below the good range? What are you setting yourself up for?

Why People Get Bad Credit

Before we answer these questions, we should identify the reasons why you will get there in the first place. You might be surprised that many of the things that you do become detrimental to your score in the long term.

It's not that you intentionally want to ruin your score. The truth is that your score is going to be influenced a lot by your very actions. As such, a crucial part of credit building is addressing your lifestyle. After all, no amount of credit-building effort will be sustainable if your lifestyle tends to undo most of the progress you have made.

As such, here are some of the reasons why credit scores can drop.

A. Late Payments

This reason is rather simple and straightforward. If you are obligated to pay an amount every month or quarter, like your utility bills and credit card dues, and you don't, then that would be a demerit on your credit history.

Of course, you can make the excuse that you lacked funds to pay off your obligations for that period. Just keep in mind that your ability to pay your bills comprises 35% of your credit score. As such, a few negative remarks on your payments will cause your score to drop in the next reporting period.

B. Defaulting

"Isn't defaulting the same as missing a payment?" You ask.

Technically, they run on the same concept. When you default, you are technically missing a payment. The difference, however, is the condition on which you miss your payment.

A person typically misses on their payment when they fail to submit the agreed money on the date that is due. For those in the lending service, that is what is called a Delinquency. It's a one-time occurrence that can be resolved if you pay what you missed on the next billing period.

A default, however, is more egregious. You can default on a payment when you miss several payments and, after demand from your lender to pay the amount you have accrued, you STILL do not make an effort to pay your dues.

To summarize: a late payment means that you just paid your dues on a date after it became due. A default, on the other hand, is when you don't pay up. At all.

Here's an example: if you miss out on paying a monthly $20.00 installment on a $500.00 loan, that is what is called delinquency. But if you miss three periods, thereby accumulating $60.00 in missed payments, and your lender has already sent you a notice demanding that you pay the past bills, then you have defaulted on your obligations.

The duration for which to call out delinquency and default is also different. Your account can get delinquency remarks for every instance that you miss a payment. But for defaults, there have to be no less than 270 days where you made no effort to pay off your debts.

While delinquencies and defaults are both negative remarks on your report, a default will hurt your credit score more. It gives lenders the impression that you are not to be subjected to any financial obligation because you suck at abiding by the terms you agreed to.

C. Charge-Off

A charge-off occurs when your creditor sees your account as a total loss. This could either mean that they have lost faith in your ability to pay off your debt or you have done something that gives them the impression that you are not going to willingly settle your accounts.

Whatever the case, a charge is meant to recuperate their losses from you by selling off your account to a collection agency. However, you still must pay your debts. It is only that you will not pay it through the original lender but to the collection agency that now controls your account.

What that means is that you can still pay off your debts and such payments will be meritoriously reported to the agency. However, that charge-off will remain as a negative remark in your report for a good seven years. That means nearly a decade of you having that remark negatively affect your score.

D. Collection Accounts

In connection to the previous cause, a collection account is made when your account changes ownership from your lender to a collection agency. That is still a negative remark on your credit score as it gives the impression that you had failed to fulfill your obligation to a lender.

So, you just have to pay your debts to the collection agency which is not a big deal, right? Technically, yes. However, what you have to understand is that collection agencies are not as lenient as most lenders.

They paid a premium for that account from the lender which means that they will resort to every possible means to compel you to pay. This includes calling your friends and family, showing up at your doorstep unannounced, and cajole you to pay up. Worse, they could file a collection lawsuit against you.

So, aside from the negative remark on your score, a collection account is often the telltale sign that you are going to get publicly dragged and humiliated by a juridical person. And the worst part is that they have every legal basis to do so.

E. Bankruptcies

The idea that everybody has is that declaring bankruptcy means that you no longer have to pay your debts. Although that is technically true, it will ultimately hurt your credit score.

Think of it this way: bankruptcy serves as your declaration to everybody else that you no longer have what it takes to pay off your debts. This will be a cause for concern for other lenders as they might find it difficult to make you pay up if they approve your loan.

As such, the presence of a bankruptcy declaration on your credit report will cause your score to go down by several hundred points. A single bankruptcy declaration is enough to make a 600 to 700 score go down to the 300 to 550 range.

And what if you declare bankruptcy but have the means to pay off your debts? That would be even worse.

Declaring bankruptcy to defraud your creditor is considered a crime in several states which can cause your credit score to go down even further. In some instances, you will also be compelled to further indemnify your creditors and serve a prison sentence.

F. Foreclosure

Foreclosures happen when you cannot pay a loan and the property you served as a security for such a loan is seized from you. As such, a foreclosure has the same effect as a default payment on your credit score.

And just like every negative remark, a foreclosure will stay on your record for 7 years or more. This gives lenders the impression that you are a high-risk person to loan money to and you have a history of missing out on your payments, deliberately or otherwise.

G. Judgments

If a lender takes you to court and the judge rules favorably on them by giving you an order to pay up, such a judgment is considered a serious demerit on your report. Judgment rendered against you in collection suits gives lenders an impression that you are not the person that will willingly pay their debts.

In other words, they would have to resort to the law just to make you pay up which makes you a risky investment. Aside from that negative impression, judges may also award damages to the creditor for anything else that you might have done against them. That means an additional obligation that you must fulfill.

[**NOTE:** These are just some of the causes that you deliberately inflict that cause damage to your credit score. However, there are also actions that you do that seem innocent but would negatively affect your rating. As such, the succeeding sections will focus on them.]

Credit Utilization

This is where a lot of credit holders unknowingly contributed to the detriment of their credit score. Credit utilization rates are simply the amount of revolving credit that you use on a particular account divided by the credit that you have.

Due to this, your credit utilization rate will be expressed in terms of percentages. For example, if you have $20,000.00 available in one credit card and you have used $5,000.00 of that amount, then your credit utilization rate is 25%. in other words, you just used a quarter of the amount of credit you are allowed to spend for that card.

Finding out your credit utilization rate is rather easy. You only have to use the formula which is stated as:

Credit Utuilization Rate = Total Debt/Available Credit

This is rather important as your credit utilization rate will be factored in the "Amount Owed" component of your credit score which contributes to 30% of your rating.

Of course, a low utilization rate simply means that you are not using much of the credit you are given. Conversely, a high rate means that you are using almost all of the credit available.

The problem is many credit holders live under the false assumption that they can just use the full amount every quarter and just pay for it later. What this impresses on any lender is that you tend to overspend and live beyond your means.

As such, a high credit utilization rate will harm your credit score. Sure, there is a lot of activity in your account but that only gives lenders the impression that you can and might spend more than what you can pay for.

So, how do you make sure that your utilization rate does not harm your credit score? Experts recommend that you stay within the 30% range. If, like the example above, you are given a $20,000.00 limit on your card, make sure your expenses do not go beyond $6,000.00 for that month.

Terminating Cards

Let us say that you have some old and unused credit cards lying around. Conventional wisdom would say that you should just close them. You're not using them anymore so doing away with them is sensible, right?
Wrong.

What you have to remember is that your credit history comprises 15% of your score. Each card you have will comprise a part of that history and closing one would effectively delete portions of that history.

For example, you have a credit history of 10 years and you just closed your first-ever credit card. That credit card was the one that started your history which means that you effectively deleted a huge chunk of your credit history. As such, you can expect your credit score to go down in the next report.

And if the cards that you close have some available balances in them, you would also increase your credit utilization rate. This is because your credit utilization rate is going to be calculated based on your total limit and your total debt owed.

For instance, you have two cards with limits at $10,000.00 each, totaling $20,000.00 all in all. For one card, you have used $5,000.00. For the other, you have used $2,000.00. In short, you have used $7,000.00 of your credits and your total rate is at 35%.

But what if you just closed one of the cards? You end up with a $10,000.00

limit and a total amount of credit used still at $7,000.00. Thus, your new utilization rate is at 70% which is way beyond the safe zone.

Credit Inquiries

There are also some credit holders out there that apply for multiple credit cards and credit lines either in quick succession or in one instance. This would initiate a hard search on your credit information which causes a slight drop in your score.

So, if one hard search drops your score slightly, what would multiple hard searches do? At worst, you can cause your score to drop by several hundred points. This is why it is recommended that you do not open more than one line of credit within a single reporting period. This way, the effects of a hard search done on your credit information will be kept to a minimum.

Side Effects

Now, what does it mean to have a bad credit score? Just being not able to enjoy the benefits of a good credit score is the beginning. There are more serious consequences that such a credit score will bring to you. They will include the following:

1. Most Lenders Will Avoid You

In recent years, banks have become stricter when approving loan applications. They do this by employing a more rigorous screening process to weed out bad applicants.

In some cases, if your score is too low for them, they will reject your application outright. Again, this has nothing to do with your character and your ability to meet the demands of the loan. It is just that your score is not giving them a lot of confidence in your ability to manage your debt.

Since most mainstream lenders will avoid you, you will have to resort to lenders that are a bit more "off the beaten path". Yes, you can still apply for loans but from lenders who are less reputable and have no compulsion to follow international banking standards.

In other words, you become a target for lenders who will impose harsh payment terms for the loan that they will give you.

2. Paying More than What You Owe

As a means to mitigate risk, lenders tend to apply high-interest rates for riskier applicants. The intention here is to either make you pay up so that you don't have to deal with your debt for far longer or so that they could squeeze out every possible mileage that they could get from your contract.

The point is that you are going to have to deal with paying more in interest if your score is decent to poor. For instance, if your score is at 500 and you apply for a $500,000.00 mortgage, you might get imposed with a 5% interest rate.

However, if you had a score of 600 to 700, that rate might be decreased somewhere between 3% to 4%. That 1-

2% difference might look insignificant but it might just help you save $100 to $200 per month. That is equal to $30,000.00 to $60,000.00 for interest rates alone over 30 years. You could have spent that amount on something more meaningful to you like sending your kids to college.

3. High Insurance Premiums

Insurance based on your credit score is a relatively new trend in the industry. However, it is a trend that many insurance providers have become more reliant on as the years passed.

In short, insurance agencies are also factoring in your spending habits in assessing the kind of risk that you will bring to them. Do not get the wrong idea, though. A sudden drop in your score will not cause your policy to get canceled or your premium to shoot up.

However, what it does is prevents you from availing of the best possible rate for your coverage. Your only solace here is that using credit scores to determine your level of risk is a practice that violates certain state consumer protection laws. In other words, it is not widely practiced around the world.

4. Career Problems

In some regions, employers can now pull up your financial records and determine whether or not to hire you, fire, promote, and demote you. As such, they could use any negative remark made by creditors as a ground to not accept your application or terminate your employment.

However, there are two major caveats. First, your employer will not get the full scope of your report without your permission. They can only get to view certain sections upon the approval of their request at the CRA.

Second, and most important of all, such inquiry to your credit information is only applicable in jobs that require transparency and fiduciary responsibility. So unless you are applying for a job that requires you to handle somebody else's money, this maneuver cannot be legally used against you.

5. Rent

As of now, you have to get at least a score of 620 to have your rent application approved by reputable landlords and property management businesses. Sure, there are some strict companies out there but you can be certain that having a score that is good to excellent will make finding a place to rent easier for you.

And if you have a poor score, you will still have some options but they are not going to be favorable to you. First, you can avail of that place but have to pay a large amount as a security deposit. Second, you can find someone to co-sign the lease for you. That way, your landlord can go after two people in case you miss some payments.
Third, and worst of all, you might just have to settle with that substandard, dingy unit in a dubious apartment complex.

6. Other Deposits

If you were to register for a service and you have a poor credit score, there is a high probability that the provider will require you to pay several months in advance as a deposit. In some cases, you will have to secure a letter of guarantee or have someone else co-sign the agreement with you.

Fortunately for you, you can't have access to utilities like electricity, water, and gas be cut off just because you have a poor credit score. Some states have implemented consumer protection laws that prevent such instances.

However, in the case of Wi-Fi and internet connection as well as cable TV, some service providers might provide some strict data usage caps or terminate your connection if you have a poor score. This is even though international laws have decreed that access to the internet is a modern human right.

7. No Credit Rewards

The general rule is that you get more perks out of your credit card if you have a high score. This will include good introductory offers as well as cash-back incentives.

There are even some credit companies that are well-connected with other businesses that you might get some perks like discounts in retail, a free mobile device, and even tickets to some concerts and sporting events.

The point is that you cannot enjoy any of these if you have a poor credit score.

8. Slow Wealth Gain

Perhaps the biggest negative effect that bad credit can inflict on your financial life is your ability to amass and save money. If you have a poor score and lenders give you high APR fees, then a lot of your money would be spent trying to pay off your debt plus the interest.

And so as long as a portion of your money is relegated to paying your debts, there will be less money to be put into equity and asset acquisition.

What you have to consider here is the Return of Investment. When you invest your money into something, you can expect that money to return to you in increments as time passes.

But with debt, there is no ROI. All that money you spend trying to deal with your interest rates could have been spent on something that will help you if you retire from your job. You could have spent it investing in a business or a hobby or to travel across the world. But you are giving away that money to satisfy the terms you signed up for with a creditor.

In Summary

Whether you perform these actions willingly or unwillingly, the fact is that there is a lot that you can do that will damage your credit score directly and indirectly. In other words, much of your lifestyle can influence how your credit score will stand in every reporting period.

That also means that you can do a lot to improve your credit score that does not involve spending money. By addressing some questionable habits of yours and making changes here and there, there is a chance that you can gradually improve on your score.

As such, the succeeding chapter will focus on you making changes in your financial habits so that lenders will give you better remarks on your score.

Chapter IV: Breaking the Debt Cycle

If much of your habits can influence your credit score, then there is no other habit more influential to your score than your tendency towards being in debt. They often say that credit holders have one of the most self-defeating lifestyles in the world and for good reason.

If you start getting in debt, chances are that you will accrue more financial obligations just to pay for your financial obligations. Being stuck in this kind of rut is thus detrimental to your score which means that getting out of the cycle is one of the most crucial steps you will ever make in your credit life.

The Pervasiveness of Debt

Is there a way to live life without incurring debt? Unless you live off the grid, then the answer is no. Borrowing money is one of the crucial steps that you could make to acquire assets or start a venture.

Unless you have saved a lot of money, chances are that you will have to live life using somebody else's just to achieve your goals. Do you want to get a degree? You sign up for a student loan. Do you plan to purchase a property? You can apply for a loan to get extra funding. Do you want a start a business, you can sign up for a loan to get the capital you need.

The point is that debt is the way of life for the modern-day consumer. Even people who have a lot of money to start with can incur debts from time to time.

Debt becomes only a problem if you cannot handle it. Being in debt means that you willingly take on an obligation to pay off what you owe when the date is due or in increments. The problem with people is that they take too many financial obligations at once. And when you take in too many debts and have a limited supply of money to pay off those debts, you initiate a toxic lifestyle under a Debt Cycle.

What is a Debt Cycle

A debt cycle is simply the never-ending process of borrowing money which eventually leads to increased expenses and the high probability of going into default.

When you spend more than what you can earn, you go into debt. And since debt comes with interest, the expenses you make increase every month to the point that whatever money you have left will be spent trying to pay off your debt.

And so what happens if you run out of money but still have debt? You start entertaining thoughts about applying for a loan just to pay off your obligations while living according to your standards.

So, in a nutshell, you can visualize the debt cycle like this:

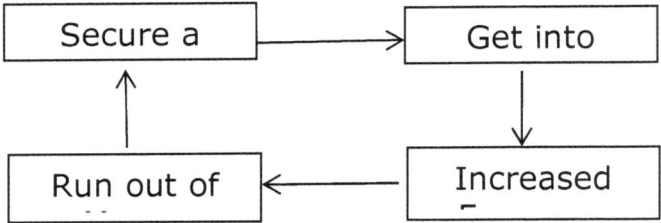

```
┌──────────────┐        ┌──────────────┐
│  Secure a    │───────▶│  Get into    │
└──────────────┘        └──────────────┘
       ▲                        │
       │                        ▼
┌──────────────┐        ┌──────────────┐
│  Run out of  │◀───────│  Increased   │
└──────────────┘        └──────────────┘
```

Here is an example to visualize the problem. Supposed that a person needs $30,000.00 to purchase a car. So, he secures a car loan with a 10-year payment term with a 5% interest rate. He could spend at least $50.00 every month plus interest to pay off his loan for the next 10 years.

But what if that person only makes $500.00 every month? 10% of his income is already relegated to paying off his car loan. What if he has other monthly expenses like:

A.	**Utilities**	**$100.00**
B.	**Groceries**	**$200.00**
C.	**Cable and Internet**	
		$ 50.00
D.	**Vehicle Maintenance**	
		$100.00
TOTAL		**$450.00**

In short, that person's monthly salary was all used up for his expenses. Now, what if he also had a $100.00 monthly charge with interest for the property he lives in, a student loan debt of $100.00 every month?

The amount he earns every month will not be enough to cover his expenses, especially his debts. As such, that person will resort to securing a loan to live decently every month while paying off his initial debts.

Debt cycles usually happen in debts that have long-term payment schemes. For instance, it is easier to fall into this cycle if you have a 30-year mortgage or a 10-year car loan. However, that is not to say that you cannot find yourself under this cycle with short-term debts. You can easily start the cycle if you take in at least 3 debts that you have to pay within a month or a year.

It does make sense to secure a loan to pay your debts. That is a valid tactic called Debt Consolidation (which you will learn more about in this book). This becomes a problem when your intention to secure a loan is mixed with the need to keep up with your lifestyle.

Getting Out of the Trap

So, is it possible to break this cycle? The answer is a YES. And the first step you have to take to get out of the cycle is to treat your condition as an actual problem. You have to admit that you are in debt and you are in the current situation you are in because of your actions. No justifications and no exhaustive reasoning as to why things happened the way they did. You are in that trap because you willingly put yourself there. Period.

Aside from that, you have to understand that your very lifestyle lends to that cycle. Even if you have enough to pay off your expenses every month, you are still staying in debt with how much of your money is being allocated for your expenses.

Moving on from where you currently are will be quite impossible if you have to maintain the cycle. As such, recognizing the need to pay off your debts ASAP is a crucial step you can make to get out of the cycle.

Once these have been set up, all you have to do is to make some important lifestyle changes which will include the following:

A. Know Your Finances

Once you know that you have a problem, the next thing to do is to find out where you exactly stand. How much income can you generate in a month? What are your sources for income/funding? Where does all that money go into?

You must establish the cash flow in your household. As such, you need to find a way to record all your expenses. You can do this by:

A. Noting all the expenses you made.
B. Keeping a copy of the receipts of every purchase.
C. Making an electronic list.
D. Getting a hold of your debit/credit card's electronic record.

This is where doing all transactions online will come in handy as they are automatically recorded. For payments that occur on a quarterly or annual basis, you might want to check on your bank or credit card provider so you will include them in your tally.

The goal here is to find out how much of your income you can afford to spend every month.

B. Craft a Spending Plan

You now have to draft a budget and follow it as accurately as possible. To do this, you have to categorize your expenses.

Firstly, you have to know what your "needs" are. These are the expenses that are essential to your survival like food and utilities. This means that such expenses are going to be your topmost priority.

Next, you have to figure out which of your expenses will come second. Since you are in debt, you should put all your current creditors here. The second group is not as essential as the first but slowly taking off these creditors from your list is crucial to you getting out of your debts.

The last category will be your "wants", the expenditures that are not necessary and satisfy only a very specific caprice of yours. This might include buying a new mobile device when you still have a functioning one or your hobbies. Even your subscription to cable TV can be considered a non-essential expense. These expenditures you can hold off on until the previous two groups have been dealt with.

C. Hold off on Credit Cards

While you are still in debt, you should fight the urge to use your credit card. Since your credit score is quite low, for now, you are bound to deal with a high-interest rate for the cards that you are using.

In other words, you are bound to pay more for every new debt that you will incur from using your credit card. While you are still trying to consolidate your income, avoid using your credit card for a while.

There are other cash-less alternatives out there that offer the same benefits of a credit card without letting you accrue new debt. This will include debit cards and other new forms of online payments.

In essence, forget that you are a credit card holder while you work in dealing with your debt.

D. Add in More Sources of Income

This move might not be risky per so but pulling it off successfully will require a bit of creativity and daring on your part. What you are going to do is to find a way to funnel in more money to yourself regularly.

Investing in a business requires a lot of capital and the ROI will take years to arrive. As such, that is out of the question (if you haven't been investing in businesses previously, of course).

Your next best bet is to find a side job or side hustle.

For example, you can get yourself registered in a ride-sharing company like Uber and ferry people from location to location on your weekends (or after your shift). You could also find odd jobs to do during the weekend.

The money you'll get from these activities will be comparatively small but they do add a considerable amount t your monthly budget. Any extra money you could make can then be used to pay for your debts so that they can be taken off your list.

E. Make Some Lifestyle Changes

Even if you don't mean it, the very activities you engage in can put a serious dent in your budget. Thus, you are more liable to overspend and get into debt. Having the occasional weekend getaway, restaurant dinner, an outing is not bad per se. However, they can ruin your budget if you do them often.

As such, you have to be more mindful of where you spend your money. You can be creative here by engaging in alternatives where you can get your fix without spending a lot. For example, if you love to sip expensive coffee at Starbucks, why not learn how to brew and mix them yourself?

The same goes for fancy dinners where you can get the same quality at home for a fraction of the cost if you know what you are doing. Better yet, you can just force your way through and say "no!" to unnecessary expenditures if you have the willpower for it.

The premise here is that you can engage in activities that will fill in a very specific need (or want) of yours without going over your monthly budget.

If you can do all of these and consistently, you can funnel in more money towards paying off your creditors. You might just get yourself debt-free within a year or so, depending on the size of your obligations.

Avoiding the Trap

Now that you know how to get yourself out of the debt cycle, conventional wisdom would say that you should do your best to avoid getting yourself stuck in the same rut in the future. Discipline and consistency are crucial here and the tips below might just help you stay out of debt for as long as humanly possible.

A. Living Below Your Means

You should start getting into a mentality of not spending money just because you can. Being a bit more conservative with where you spend your money is going to help you here.

For example, if you plan to purchase a house, choose the one that you can afford NOW than the one you need a loan for. And if you live within a bus route with available units from sunrise to midnight, why choose the option where you have to apply for a car loan?

Essentially, you have to find a way where you can earn more and spend less. This does not mean that you have to forego quality and safety just because you are a cheapskate. Instead, you must know where to spend where it matters.

B. Never, Ever, Get the Maximum Loan

Always consider these: lenders, no matter how friendly you think they are, will always have their best interests FIRST. For example, if a mortgage lender allows you to borrow the maximum purchase price to afford that home, do you think that they did it out of the goodness of their heart or because they think you are a nice guy? No.

More often than not, they allowed you to borrow the full price so that they can earn more from you in the long term. If you have to apply for a loan, make sure that you already have amassed at least 50% of the purchasing price of that property/car/business. This way, you only have to deal with a smaller debt which you can clear off in a shorter period.

C. Have Contingencies

Aside from the debt that you incur from your everyday expenses, there will also be unforeseen circumstances that would end with owing money to somebody else. This might include paying for hospital bills because you or somebody else you dearly love gets sick or your house needing emergency repairs because of a fire/break-in/accident.

Indeed, you cannot predict these things and completely avoid them when they happen. However, you can avoid getting yourself in debt because of these sudden expenses by saving money at the side.

At this point, you should save up for an emergency fund by putting in a bit of what you earn every month into a special account. That way, you have a bit of money to use in case the need arises for you to spend on something crucial.

There is no hard and fast rule as to how much you should save for emergencies. However, it is recommended that your standing emergency fund should always be three to six times more than what your current monthly income is.

Signing yourself up for insurance will also work. Sure, you might be spending for the coverage but the amount you will get for indemnification will be considerable enough to address your needs should they arise.

To Summarize

Debt is one of the more serious problems you need to address before you could start fixing your credit score. Much of its problem comes from the fact that it is habit-forming by nature. In essence, your way of living can serve to be a detriment to your credit score and your financial stability.

By learning how to get out of the cycle of debt and stay out for as long as possible, you can start making more mindful changes in your financial activities. And when it comes to repairing your credit score, there is still quite a lot to address, fix, and change.

Chapter V: Securing Loans

As was previously stated, only a very select few can truly call themselves free from the credit system. For regular people (and even some influential individuals), there is the need to find a loan and get the funding needed for a major investment.

As of now, there are two major sources to get the funding: Bank or Broker.

This does beg the question: which of these two options is the best for you.

Do remember that even while you are trying to repair your credit, there might come a time when you will need to apply for a loan.

With that being said, both banks and brokers are viable options. For the option that will truly meet your needs without ruining your credit score even further, you might have to look at a few considerations.

How Either Option Works

Since both options are viable, what makes them different from one another? Would it matter if you get your loan from a bank or a broker?

The answer is yes and the option that you will pick will be dependent on what you need or, to be franker about it, what you are willing to put up with.

Before anything else, you must understand that both banking and brokerage systems follow a strict set of guidelines. Without policies in place, they cannot hope to make a dime out of each person that borrows money from them.

In other words, loaning from a bank or a broker will follow a strict yet flexible process structure. This will give you an idea as to how you are going to fair with the contract you are signing yourself up for.

A. **Banks**

By their very nature, banks have a self-sustaining funding system. In other words, they use their own money to finance all transactions they enter into.

As far as their structure is concerned, every person who takes a part in the loaning process answers to the banking entity. This includes the loan officers, underwriters, and processors.

Arguably, the most valuable person in this structure is the loan officers who are tasked with finding the funds necessary to support the bank's operations. In short, the loan officers ensure that there is a flow of cash going in and out of the bank. Of course, it is incoming cash flow that is the most important of the two.

Due to their work, the loan officers get the most from originating loans and can dictate the prices that the bank charges for each loan.

Due to the self-sustaining nature of a bank, you can be certain that the people there will be selling you THEIR product. However, a bank may adopt a more flexible scheme for pricing so applicants can choose from different price points. There might be loans with cheap starting rates that go high as the years pass and there are loans with rates that do not change for years.

B. Brokers

The best way to describe a broker is that they are independent agents. They might be smaller in terms of size and scope compared to a bank, a broker more than makes up for it with the sheer volume of options that they can offer.

When you ask a broker for a loan, they can offer you not only one product line but several ones coming from different banks. If the rates of the loan they offer are high, they might offer a rebate to pay off costs on behalf of the borrower as well as their commission.

But for low rates, the broker will only ask for the commission in between 1% to 3% of the loan's total price. Without that commission, the broker earns absolutely nothing from every transaction they engage in.

Pros and Cons

At a glance, you can see that banks and brokers operate under very different systems. As such, each option will yield to your very different sets of advantages and disadvantages

Banks

If you were to apply for a loan at a bank, you could take advantage of several perks which include:

A. Legally-Mandated Hand Holding

As required by law, the bank must work with you at every stage of the loaning process. This means that you will deal with the same loaning officer and agents from the start of the loan until you paid your last installment. Of course, this is provided that nothing happens that would change the agreement you have with the bank.

Of course, this means that the loan officer is required to explain to you the nature of your obligation as well as the implications for each term you will sign up for. At the very least, this prevents you from putting yourself in a situation where you sign up for something you didn't understand.

This will be beneficial to you as you could build rapport with the loaning officer especially if you diligently pay your dues. The closer you will get to the loaning officer, the easier it will be for you to control how and when you can pay for the dues.

This might even help you with your credit score as the loan officer might hold off on reporting any payment you missed or defaulted on. The key operative word here, of course, is "might".

B. Comparatively Lower Pricing

The biggest factor you have to deal with as a debtor would be the interest. With banks, however, the prices that they offer would be comparatively lower than what brokers can provide, and that even includes interest.

This is because you are directly paying the bank with each installment. There is no commission to be paid since there is no middleman to speak of when dealing with a bank directly.

In practice, this should help you save on the initial payment you will make for the loan.

C. Better Customer Experience

Compared to what brokers can offer, a bank will follow a standardized process when it comes to offering financing options that the applicant needs and can manage. They will take their time understanding what kind of loan would work well with you while also allowing you a bit of leeway to negotiate your payment terms.

You have to consider the fact that banks can sustain themselves. They don't need your contract to live for another moment and, as such, would not hurry you to make a decision. All that matters for them is for you to make a decision when the time is right to start a relationship that the bank can profit from.

Of course, these advantages will be off-set by several downsides which include:

A. Semi-Transparency

Sure, a bank is required to help you through every step of the loaning process. However, they are not mandated to tell you exactly how much they are going to make from your loan. Sure, they will tell you the exact fees and costs for your loan but they will not go out of their way to explain this to you unless you ask.

Aside from some filial issue, this semi-transparent nature of the bank when it comes to their potential earnings with you would imply that you might end up paying more from your interest. And you'd be none the wiser for it.

B. Limited Options

As was stated a few paragraphs ago, a bank would sell you their products ONLY. At best, the loan officer can give you financing options directly offered by the bank or some affiliated program. As such, you can only get a handful of options from a bank compared to the veritable portfolio's worth of offers that a broker can offer.

C. Stricter Approval Process

Now, this is where your credit score will come into play. Banks can approve or reject your loan depending on your score. They might approve your loan with a manageable interest rate if the score is high or set you with a strict interest rate if your score is low if they even approve of it.

But here's the more frustrating part: there are times when the bank can forego your credit score entirely. Even if your score is good, the bank might reject your application in favor of an applicant that they are more familiar with.

There are many reasons for these. Perhaps the bank has strict in-house policies and guidelines. Perhaps they look into other factors aside from your credit score when deciding on your loan. Or perhaps they just don't trust you because you are a stranger to them.

Either way, you can expect that a bank might approve or reject your loan for reasons that only they would know.

Brokers

If you do choose a broker, you can take advantage of the following perks which are:

A. Better Selection

Because brokers are independent, they can serve as one-stop shops for those looking for financing options. A single broker can offer you multiple product lines coming from various banks. This, at the very least, will help you save time as you don't have to move from one broker to another just to get the best option for you.

This advantage should not be underestimated as there is a chance that a broker can help you find a financing option that is specialized for your needs. At best, they will know of a lender that has an offer that will match your needs and your paying power.

B. Flexible Pricing

Brokers take the more "customer-friendly" approach to pricing as you can haggle payment terms with them. This is because a broker will set their profit margin and payment terms which allow applicants to pick and choose which payment option they are most comfortable with.

C. Transparency

Unlike banks, brokers are required by law to tell you exactly how much they are going to earn from the transaction. They are even required by law to explain to you how they came up with such prices and what elements are to be included in determining your payment terms.

And, as with banks, brokers do have some drawbacks which are as follows:

A. No Procedural Assurance

You have to remember that the broker will still have to submit your application to the primary lender. As such, they have no control as to how long the approval process will take. They can't even assure you that your loan will be approved as that is the lender's prerogative.

For instance, you picked this loan option from a broker, provide the broker with the requirements they were asking for, and the broker will submit the papers to the lender. Once it is in the lender's hands, you can only hope that your application gets approved. The worst-case scenario is that the lender would forget that an application was submitted to their office.

B. A More Complicated (And Expensive) Process

Brokers act as middle agents which means that the process of securing a loan will now have additional steps for you to complete. Of course, the added complexity will increase the long-term costs on your part.

What if you were paired with a broker who cannot properly explain to you the lender's loaning process? Chances are that your application will be rejected multiple times until you get it right. With a bank, you can know if your application was approved or rejected quickly and with little cost on your part.

C. Longer Closing Time

And since brokers are not connected to the bank offering the loan, the time it takes to complete your application is a bit longer. There is no assurance that you will get the loan that you need within weeks or a month after submitting the requirements.

This would be a problem if you need that money ASAP. What if, for example, you are trying to secure a loan to purchase a parcel of land within a month or so? If you apply for a loan at a broker, the deal might be closed before your loan gets approved.

Bank or Broker?

So which option is the best for you? There is no standard to follow when it comes to picking between a bank or a broker for your loan.

However, either option can be viable for you if there are certain conditions. If your loan is to be used for a simple and straightforward purpose and you have a particularly strong credit score assessment, then a bank is highly recommended as a loaning option.

However, if certain impediments could complicate the loaning process like a bad FICO score, you might find a broker to be a bit more sympathetic as an option.

For instance, let us say that your current score is at 500. There is no assurance that a bank would even take a look at your application especially if they have no previous transactions with you. As such, your options for mainline financial products are going to be limited provided that you are allowed to choose in the first place.

However, a broker might help you secure a loan while you are still repairing your score and with reasonable rates. They would know which lenders are lenient when it comes to applicants with bad credit scores.

As such, you have to ask yourself this question when looking for a loan: what do you value the most.

If you are the person that looks for loaning options that are safer with minimal variables, then you should consider applying for a loan at a bank. But if you favor leniency and assistance while you are doing your part in recovering your credit score, then a broker might be the more sensible option.

Either way, you should ask around first before you make a decision. This is because banks and brokers are not the only funding option that you might encounter out there.

Chapter VI: Predatory Lending

As of now, you should get the impression that lenders are in it for themselves. No matter how friendly they approach you or how good they are in making you comfortable, every move they make is calculated to serve their primary goal: profit.

That being said, lenders are required by law to be FAIR. They are tasked to ensure that your consumer rights are not violated and you are not placed in a position where you can easily fall into a debt cycle, regardless of your character.

And when they conduct their operations without any consideration on your welfare, that lender becomes predatory by nature.

So what is predatory lending, then? The simplest definition is that predatory lending pertains to any practice by lenders intended to mislead, induce, and force lenders into taking loans.

Aside from that, the loans themselves must be accompanied by unreasonable payment terms and interest rates that are not up to industry standards.

Predatory lenders take advantage of your circumstances and lack of knowledge with regards to industry practices to place you in a debt cycle that becomes toxic as time passes, or worse.

So predatory lenders are those loan sharks and mafiosos you see on the TV, right? Technically, that would be true. Any collecting agency whose practices are not in line with what the industry has determined to be a standard is a predatory lender.

However, even more, legitimate lenders can become predatory by their policies. A predatory lender can come in the form of a bank, a financial company, a broker, and even attorneys.

How to Spot a Predatory Lender

There is no standard as to what constitutes a predatory lending entity. However, these ruthless lenders do share some qualities and practices which are easy to spot if you look hard enough.

1. TGTBT: Too Good To be True

You can easily spot a predatory lender by the way they make their offer. They focus too much on your convenience. And this is not just convenience but the kind of convenience where your risk exposure is completely removed and the speed at which your loan is approved is nearly instant.

Common predatory tactics include promises like the ability to repair your score with each payment, settling your debt for less than what you initially owed, and a full loan price despite your poor credit score.

Normally, no lender would give any other benefit to their loan aside from the money that is being transacted. You are not supposed to enjoy perks as a loan is an obligation by definition. And when an obligation starts being marketed as less than cumbersome, your mental alarms should start ringing.

2. Downplayed Fees and Penalties

A predatory lender also sweetens the deal by not talking about certain things like, for example, fees. They might downplay the costs by the way they present the loan or keep such expenses hidden from you through vaguely-worded terms in your agreement.

And when you discover these fees, you will find them to be excessive. For instance, you might be imposed with a penalty for prepaying your loan or get charged with more than the industry limit of 5% of the actual loan price.

What makes this egregious is that the penalties artificially inflate your Annual Percentage Rate. At their very worst, these penalties and fees can increase your balance by 200% to 400%.

3. Balloon Payments

To make your monthly payment look low, predatory lenders often ask for repayment at the end of the term. The problem is that the amount you will have to pay is more than what you are owed. This is what is called balloon payments and predatory lenders use this to give credit holders a false impression that their debt will be manageable.

Also, balloon payments make for the perfect setup for another trap. Since the amount is now more than what you borrowed, you are forced to refinance. As such, you incur new debt or have to default on your loan.

4. Loan Flipping

You will notice that predatory lenders are less hesitant in having you borrowing money while your initial loan has yet to be cleared. This incurs additional fees on your part which makes your debt even more unmanageable.

In essence, you could tell that a lender is predatory if they encourage you to stay in debt, not out of it.

5. Asset-Based Lending

Usually, a lender will grant or reject your loan based on your ability to pay for it. As such, you should be wary of those who grant loans based on what you have.

For example, a standard lender will ask you for your monthly income statements and other financial documents to determine whether or not you can repay the loan. However, a predatory lender will look at expensive things that you own.

One prime example of this is a title-based loan. To secure the loan, you might have to surrender your title to real or personal property like your car or your home. If you can't repay the loan, the lender can repossess your property.

If your lender starts pushing you to use your real or personal property as a security for your loan, you need to walk away from that deal as quickly as possible.

6. Steering

Again, the orientation of the lender comes into play here. A good lender will recommend to you the loan plan that fits your needs and paying power. A predatory lender, on the other hand, will insist on one type of product over the other.

You can easily tell this by the way the commandeer the conversation. A predatory lender will always point towards you signing up for that loan whereas more reputable lenders will allow you time to think through your decision.

7. Subprime Loans

Mortgages are where a lot of predatory lenders operate in. This is because home loans have to be backed by real property which makes it easier for a predatory lender to profit not only from the loan but from the sale of the property in case the credit holder defaults.

Here's the catch, however: subprime loans are not predatory per se. Higher interest rates are there to make sure that the lender's exposure to risk coming from a person with a poor credit score is lessened.

It is just that predatory lenders use these loans as a shield against scrutiny.

8. Negative Amortization

Negative amortization happens when the lender allows you to pay for less of the cost in monthly interest. After this, they will then add the outstanding amount in interest to your total loan balance.

What happens then is that your loan balance grows while your interest rate remains the same. So, instead of taking off chunks from your loan, you are adding more. This means that the duration of your obligation increases and you are indebted to the lender for more.

9. Packed Loans

To sweeten the deal, the lender might offer you perks that are not necessary. This usually comes in the form of a service like credit insurance where you can be covered by an insurance plan of sorts for your loan.

What makes this highly dubious is that it adds more fees to your balance. After all, you will have to continuously subscribe to the service to enjoy its benefits.

Again, packing a loan with services is not illegal. It only becomes highly suspect when the lender pushes that you also subscribe to the service aside from your loan.

10. Zero Credit Checks

If your credit score is quite low, a lender who will not check on your credit score would like a godsend. However, in most cases, it is a major indicator that they will try to rip you off.

Think of it this way: any lender would want to make sure that they know who they are dealing with so they wouldn't be wasting money. Also, credit checks are inexpensive tools to help a lender identify the amount of risk they will be exposed to if they do business with you.

So why would a lender easily part with their money and give it to someone they know absolutely nothing about? If a lender tells you that they are not interested in your credit standing and will give you a loan anyway, it is recommended that you do no further business with them.

It all goes back to the oft-repeated phrase "If it's too good to be true, it usually is".

Avoiding Predators

In as much as these lenders are aggressive and ruthless, they are rather easy to avoid or, if encountered, dealt with. To do so, here are a few tips to keep in mind.

A. Know the Red Flags

The practices above are some of the ways that lenders have managed to put credit holders in severe debt cycles. However, these lenders are quite crafty and would change tactics from time to time.

To spot a predatory lender, ask yourself the following questions:

- Is the lender being honest with the fees and penalties?
- Is the lender looking at my credit report, no matter how bad it is?

- Would a stricter lender offer me the same terms and interest rates?
- Are the lender's repayment terms geared towards credit building/recovery/repair and not for my "convenience"?
- Did the lender ask for my financial information and not for my assets?

If the answer to all of these is a "no", then it is highly likely you are dealing with a predatory lender. As such, you are better not entertaining their offer.

A. Look for More Options

A tried-and-tested tactic that you can use is to shop around before you close a deal. This might be a tough hurdle for you to overcome if you have been handled by legitimate lenders poorly in the past but you have to seek more options.

The goal here is to compare offers and find a commonality between all lenders. If the practices of one lender stick out like a sore thumb, then you have identified who to avoid.

B. Consider Some Alternatives

There are other funding options out there that do not require you to put your credit score at risk. This could include lending money from friends and family (note: do pay them on the due date for the sake of your relationship), charity programs, and public assistance services.

So, are you begging for money? The answer, technically, is yes.

However, the blow to your ego notwithstanding, these options are the only way you can get money without harming your credit score. And this is rather crucial at this point since you are still trying to repair your credit score.

By using alternative funding options, you can get the money you need to live for another month without the risk of another demerit on your credit report.

Why Awareness Matters

So, why talk about predatory lenders when the focus of the book is on repairing your credit score? The simple reason is that the primary prey of these lenders is those with a poor credit score.

When your score drops to a considerable degree, you are bound to have limited options when it comes to funding. You would be looking for a more lenient lender and understanding of your situation.

And this is what predatory lenders are looking for: people who will leap on any offer given to them willingly. They will bombard you with very aggressive sales tactics that will compel you to sign up for the loan.

And once you do take them up on your offer, you will be imposed with a payment term that you cannot hope to manage in the long run.

The worst part about this is that these lenders are still entitled to report you to the CRAs for every payment you missed. And, aside from that, some predatory lenders might resort to less-than-legal means to make you pay up which includes threats of violence and public humiliation.

The point is that predatory lenders can place you in a situation that you will have no means of escape but through paying what you owe plus the interest.

However, such situations are easy to avoid if you know what to look for.

Chapter VII: Checking on Your Credit Report

You have to get familiar with your credit report to properly repair your score. Remember that your score is just a numerical representation of your impression of lenders.

A report, on the other hand, will provide the details as to why a lender should trust you with their money or not. Also, lenders would want to look at the specifics in your credit report to support their decision to either approve or reject your application.

As such, you should know what credit reports might tell you or anybody else reading them. Don't worry, what is contained in the credit report is not as complicated as you might think it is. It only requires you to know what to look for and then act on such information.

What's Included in Your Credit Report?

Every CRA will prepare a report for credit holders. This would only mean that your credit report from Experian would look considerably different from what TransUnion and Equifax have prepared for you.

With that being said, you should expect your credit report to include vital information like:

A. Personal Information - This is rather basic as it contains your name, current address, and contact information. Aside from that, this section would contain any alias you use with your creditors as well as any misspelling given by creditors when they report you to the CRA.

Besides, your personal information would include your former and current employment, the contact numbers of your employers, and even your social security number. All of this is to help a lender learn all that they could about your financial standing.

However, your report will not include personal information like your level of education, the balance in your bank account, and your monthly income. Generally speaking, the name of your spouse will not even be included here if you are married. The only that the identity of your spouse will be included in the report is if the creditor specifically reports them especially if you are solidarily liable for the debt.

B. Accounts – This will contain all the active accounts that you have which would include loans, credit cards, and mortgages. Also, this will list the creditors that you are currently indebted to, the status of your financial obligations to your lenders (whether paid, active, or defaulted), balances, payment history, and account numbers.

As you could already tell, this is the part that lists all of the positive and negative remarks made by lenders about you. If you missed a payment, defaulted on your debts, or tend to pay past the due date, this will be laid out here for future lenders to discover.

Of course, this will tell lenders if you can handle another obligation especially if you already are indebted to a handful of lenders. Naturally, they'd prefer if you have current active balances so you can prioritize paying your debts to them.

C. Public Records - What will be included here are references to documents about you that are publicly available. This will include court judgments in collection cases where you are the defendant, declarations of bankruptcies, and even your registration in the local electoral roll.

D. Inquiries - This part will list all of the inquiries recently made about your financial information. This will include the identity of the person making the inquiry, when such inquiry was made, and whether the inquiry falls under a hard or a soft search.

Is Reporting Your Activities Mandatory?

Generally speaking, no. In as much as they can disregard a score on your report, a lender can also choose not to report any unfavorable action you have made. We could chalk this up to you building rapport with them or the lender is not too bothered with reporting you yet as they might give you the benefit of the doubt.

Either way, no law requires creditors to report you to the CRAs for every transaction you make or payment you complete. And if they do, they can choose to submit such data to at least 2 of the 3 CRAs.

This could lead to you having slightly different scores from the three reporting agencies. However, the difference in your scores with the CRAs is not so wide that you might get a favorable one in Experian and a poor score with Equifax and TransUnion.

Who Can Check on Your Credit

Report

If you think about it, a credit report can act as a public document. After all, you are not the one preparing it and those who meet the requirements can secure a copy for themselves.

But that's the point: the general public has no access to your credit report even if they want to check on your data. Different state consumer protection laws limit access to your credit information to a few individuals which would include:

A. You

Since this is information about your activities, you are entitled to a copy of your credit report upon request. Also, credit score checks made by the person to which the information pertains would rarely affect their credit score.

B. Lenders

Whenever you apply for a loan, the lender would then check on your credit report to make a decision. This is what is called a "hard search" which can affect your credit score greatly if done in quick succession.

To be granted a copy of your report, the lender must first seek permission. As such, they would ask you if they could be given a copy of your report by the reporting agency.

C. Landlords

This is a new trend but landlords are now pulling credit reports before they allow tenants to settle in a unit that they own. Rent is not strictly a form of credit but it can work like one since you are asking that person to allow you to use a part of their premises with the consideration that you will pay for such usage every month for a set time.

Due to the nature of your contract with a landlord, they are entitled to ask for a copy of your report from the CRA. Of course, they cannot get a copy of such without your express permission.

D. Other Authorized Persons

If you apply for a job, an employer can ask to review your credit report. However, this is only possible if you are applying for a job that imposes fiduciary responsibilities like handling money or private documents.

Also, insurers and service providers can ask for your credit report as their line of work involves trusting you to continually pay for whatever they have to offer. Of course, these three persons can only get a copy of your report upon your consent.

Understanding Your Report

A credit report is prepared and laid out in a way that it is easy for you to pick out the bits of information that you need. That being said, it can be daunting to sift through all of that information and properly interpret what it is trying to say to you.

Also, you need to know if the credit report is 100% correct and dispute whatever improper data it contains. As such, you'd have to know how to properly look at your credit report. Here's how:

1. Get the Basics Right

A mistake that many people make is that they gloss over the basic information in their reports. You might think that data like your name, address, social security number, and contact information are window dressing but they could affect your credit score.

For starters, check if your name is correct or is 100% referencing you. If you have a rather generic name like "Bob Smith", there is a 100% chance that the CRA would mistake you for 5 other Bob Smiths in the area. As such, entries between you and your namesakes can be mistakenly attributed to one another.

To prevent this, make sure that everything in your basic information is correct. If you have a suffix like "Jr." or a roman numeral, make sure that is included there. You could also avoid cases of mistaken identity by checking if the social security number is listed in your report is yours.

Also, check the addresses there and make sure you lived there. If you haven't set foot in Wisconsin or Edinburgh before, make sure that such addresses are not included in your information.

2. Mind Your History

This will be the most extensive part of your activity as this is where almost all errors are made in your credit report. Go through every reported transaction there, check the date, and note who was the business/creditor you were transacting with.

At the same time, look for what was not included. For example, you might have completed a loan but your report still marks that account as active with a pending balance. This means that your last payment was not reported.

More importantly, take note of what credits were opened or transactions made that you have no recollection of. This is a telltale sign that you are a victim of identity theft and you need to report such to the authorities ASAP.

As for erroneous entries, there is a dispute process that you can initiate which we will discuss in detail later.

3. Public Records

As far as this section is concerned, errors are a rare occurrence. Just make sure that you go through this part and check if they should still be there.

What you have to remember is that negative records like judgments and tax liens should only stay in your report for at least 7 years and no more than 10 years. If you have a decade-old entry in this section, you need to have it cleared immediately.

4. Check for Hard Searches

As was stated, a single hard search causes a slight drop in your score. Multiple ones done within a short period are bound to decrease your score considerably.

Whenever you see a hard search recorded in your report, just check if you consented to that inquiry. If not, the CRA can remove that entry in your report which should raise your score a bit.

And if you did consent to the hard searches, you must keep in mind that they should stay in your report for no more than 2 years. If you have a hard search in your report that is more than

24 months old, notify your CRA to have it removed quickly.

Other Notable Entries

There are also some little icons and remarks in your credit report that you might not be familiar with. The first of these is what we call "Open Account". As the term would imply, an open account is simply a type of account that you have not yet closed.

All your active credit accounts fall under this category but they would also include the accounts that you forgot to close but are no longer using.

For instance, you might have opened a credit card a few years ago but no longer use them in favor of a newer account. So as long as you did not terminate that account, it will remain with an open status in your credit history.

Open accounts are generally harmless so as long as they do not have any outstanding balance. Also, closing an open account might be detrimental to your credit history if that account contains years' worth of paid-off transactions. But if the account is empty and useless, you should have it closed.

Another term you might encounter is the letter "U". This simply means "unclassified" which means that there is an error in the entry of your information. Most likely, there are discrepancies in the collection or an internal error with the creditor's payment system.

If that account is new, the U would also signify that there haven't been any payments made to it yet. Either way, this indication is harmless and can be easily amended.

Can Somebody Inquire for My Data Without Asking Me First?

Technically speaking, yes. The need to get your consent is a requirement only for a hard search. This means that the CRA would go out of their way to pull out your credit data and prepare a fresh report which takes time.

However, there is also something that we call a "soft" search. Perhaps the lender is only looking for your basic information and other specific bits of data in your credit report. This would not be time-consuming for a CRA to do and will not impact your credit score.

As such, the lender can do a soft search on you without having to ask for your consent. It is just that the data they will receive will not be a complete picture of your credit standing.

Disputing a Report

Whenever you find an erroneous entry in your report, you are well within your rights to dispute it. After all, that report will be your resume of sorts to a lender and the wrong entry can give the wrong impression of that person.

This will initiate a process wherein the CRA will investigate your claim and perform actions in response to what they find. If there are no errors, the CRA will explain to you exactly why that entry was interpreted in that manner.

If there was something wrong, the CRA will then make the necessary amendments and adjust your score. This will take a few days to a week but you won't have to wait for long to get an amended report.

The Dispute Process

Each CRA will have its dispute resolution process. However, disputes generally follow the same three steps which are.

1. Making a Claim

When you believe that there is something wrong with your credit report, you can submit a letter to request an investigation of your data. The letter should be straightforward enough to make but, if you are a bit lacking in creativity, there are templates that you can follow *(more on these later)*

Some agencies like TransUnion also allow you to draft your complaint online. But nothing beats the formality and sincerity that a letter could offer. Either way, you have options in drafting a letter to the CRA whose report you are disputing.

2. Verification

Upon receipt of your request, the CRA will then contact the creditor/business from which the error originated and verify your claim. Verification only happens when the error is quite substantial that the CRA has no other option but to clarify to the creditor what happened in that entry.

However, for more formal errors like typos in your name or the wrong social security number, the agency can do away with the verification process.

3. Amendment

If the creditor does confirm that the entry was an error, the agency is then required to make the necessary adjustments to your data and your score. If the entry was true and correct, no revisions will be made.

Either way, the agency will send you a summary of the investigation and inform you when you will receive an amended copy.

Now, what happens if after the dispute, there are still errors found in your report or new ones were made? You can easily initiate another dispute process and the agency will then have to make the necessary adjustments.

Do this as often as you can until you get the most accurate version of your report.

Important: Although you are entitled to dispute your report, you cannot dispute your actual score. Your score will be tabulated based on the data that the agency receives from your creditors. In essence, formulating your score is a purely mathematical process free of any human intervention save for the actual input of data.

As such, if you feel that your score is wrong, you have to find the actual error in your report. As changes are made in your data, the score will automatically adjust itself. Depending on what was changed, you might see a change by a handful of points to hundreds.

Chapter VIII: The 609

Aside from the internal dispute process of each CRA, you can also legally compel an agency to provide you with accurate credit information to amend your report.

This is where a 609 Letter would come into play. It is quite understandable if you some apprehensions about drafting a complaint letter. What should you include? What is the purpose of your letter? How do you even make an introduction to the CRA?

To make things easier for you, you should follow a template. This is where the 609 Letter comes into play as it is the standard letter for disputing entries in your credit report.

The 609 Letter is derived from Section 609 of the Fair Credit Reporting Act which is an extensive provision on what credit holders can use if they feel that there is something wrong in their reports.

In essence, Section 609 of the FCRA states that every credit holder has a right to a copy of their credit report and the information contained within it. If the information cannot be verified, then it must be removed from your report.

Some companies have made a business offering copies of 609 templates for consumers. But here's the kicker: it's actually for free. A 609 letter would look something like this:

SAMPLE 609 Letter

(Name)
(Address)
(Contact Number)

(Date)

Subject: Fair Credit Reporting Act, Section 609

Dear (Credit Reporting Agency)

I am exercising my right under the Fair Credit Reporting Act under Section 609 to request information

on the following items listed in my credit report:

1. (Insert Creditor Name), (Insert Account Number), (Insert Date)
2. (Insert Creditor Name), (Insert Account Number), (Insert Date)
3. (Insert Creditor Name), (Insert Account Number), (Insert Date)

As per Section 609, I am entitled to see the sources of information which are the original contracts that contain my signature for each creditor.

My identify information is as follows:

(Date Of Birth)
(Social Security Number)
(Optional: Contact Information of your Legal Representative)

As proof of my identity, I have contained herein copies of (documents to prove your identity).

If you are unable to verify the information contained in my most recent report, the information

should be removed from my report within 30 days.

Sincerely,

(You)
To further inspire your creativity, here are some more templates that you can follow:

Example A

Manuel Rios
123 Point Avenue, Las Vegas, Nevada 93746-2836

January 23, 2019

Subject: Fair Credit Reporting Act, Section 609

Dear Experian,

I, Manuel Rios, am exercising my right under the Fair Credit Reporting Act under Section 609 to request information on the following items listed in my credit report:

1. 924 Corp. G-983765 December 08, 2018
2. Core Fitness Co. 96-47361 November 2, 2018
3. Sunlight Industries, Inc. 25-98371 November 3, 2018

As per Section 609, I am entitled to see the sources of information which are the original contracts that contain my signature for each creditor.

My identify information is as follows:

Date of Birth: July 23, 1987
SSN: 3837-99328213A

Legal Representative: Tyson Stewart, JD
Attorney Roll No. 80-983271NV

As proof of my identity, I have contained herein copies of my birth certificate, passport, social security card, and driver's license.

If you are unable to verify the information contained in my most recent report, the information should be removed from my report within 30 days.

Sincerely,

(Signed)
Manuel Rios

Example B

Stella Marie Williams
123 Street, Fond Du Lac, Wisconsin
203-517321

December 19, 2020

Subject: Fair Credit Reporting Act, Section 609

Dear TransUnion,

Having carefully gone over your report on my credit activities, I am exercising my right under the Fair Credit Reporting Act under Section 609 to request amendments on the following entries.

Creditor Name	Account Number	Reason for Dispute
X-Travaganza, Inc.	98-28181	I do not recall opening an

		account with this company
Unwell Corp.	M-267251	Entry marked as open when I have terminated my account with them
Aerobics Fit n Jazz	9821-32766156	Account already paid in full but outstanding balance is still present

As per Section 609, I am also entitled to see the sources of information which are the original contracts that contain my signature for each creditor.

My identify information is as follows:

Date of Birth: August 9, 1998
SSN: 87-9891827512

Legal Representative: Ceres Olivier, LLB

Attorney Roll No.   78-09371651WN

As proof of my identity, I have contained herein copies of the following:
- Birth certificate
- Driver's license
- Passport
- Receipts of bills from Aerobics Fit N Jazz and Unwell Corp.
- Social security card

Please do verify and amend the entries. If they are not verified, they should be removed from my credit report as soon as possible.

Sincerely,

(Signature)
Stella Marie Williams

Example C

Arthur Kingston
87A Street, New York City, New York
465-093175

February 2, 2021

Subject: Fair Credit Reporting Act, Section 609

Dear Equifax,

In my recent credit report from your office, I noticed some errors. They are as follows:

1. **ABC Corp.**
Account No: G-202815
Date Opened: 11-09-2020

Dispute Reason: I can't recall opening such an account with this company.

2. Simon Says Realty Corp.
Account No: 98-284756
Date Opened: January 9, 2010

Dispute Reason: I already completed my loan with the company and have left my apartment unit since November 10, 2020. The account should already be marked as closed as of November 15, 2020.

3. **Big Mike's Auto Emporium**
Account No:89-2817

Dispute Reason: I already paid my balance with them last September 10, 2020. The account should have no outstanding balance anymore.

As per section 609 of the Fair Credit Reporting Act, I am entitled to have erroneous and unverified statements removed from my account.

My identity information is as follows:

Date of Birth: January 23, 1991
Social Security Number: 010-48921475

As further proof of my identity, I have also attached herewith several copies of the following documents:

- Birth certificate
- Social security card
- Passport
- Driver's license
- Cellphone utility bill

Under the Fair Credit Reporting Act, any entry in my report should be removed by your office within 30 days upon verification. Thank you for your consideration.

Sincerely,

(Signed)
Arthur Kingston

When writing your dispute letter, it is also necessary that you affix a copy of your credit report while highlighting whatever alleged error you discovered. As for the number of copies that you must prepare, the standard is four for each document attached to the letter.

If the same accounts are being reported to all the CRAs, you must send different dispute letters containing the pertinent documents to each.

Also, to make sure that the CRA gets the letter, you have to send them via certified mail with a return receipt being requested. If you send your mail through the post office, you will have to pay $8.00 for each packet which is a rather small price to pay to get your report corrected.

Also, they might ask for copies of your personal information as well as your credit report. However, they will write the letter and even send it to the CRAs on your behalf.

Once the letter is sent, all that is left to do is to wait for the response of the agency. You should get the amen

What a 609 Can Do

As the letter is compliant with the FCRA, a 609 will allow you to request the following:

- Information coming from your credit files.
- The source from which that information was derived.
- The identity of the people who have accessed your credit report in the past.
- The number of hard and soft searches done on your credit information for the last year or so.

This does beg the question: Does a 609 Letter work?

What you have to remember is that the FCRA mandates all credit reporting agencies to report only the information that is verified. By asking for copies and sources of your credit information, you give the agency the chance to trace their work and make the necessary amendments.

And this is not just any information that can be easily reproduced or simulated. Things like the original copy of the credit application that you signed are a bit hard to find as no less than 5 copies of that document could exist at any given time. As such, the chances that a disputed entry can be verified is quite low.

However, that does not mean you are no longer required to pay any legitimate debt under that account. If the information is removed or amended, you are still obligated to pay whatever outstanding balance you have with your creditors.

As for repairing your credit score, a 609 letter is not the better or inferior alternative to the standard dispute process. It merely exists as another option that you can take to correct errors in your credit report.

If there would be one flaw with a 609 dispute, it would be the fact that the FCRA never required credit bureaus to keep proof of debt or any signed contract. As such, there is still a sliver of a chance that the information can still be verified.

This is where the standard dispute process will be more effective as this would compel the agency to manually verify the entry with the creditor.

The point is that there is no assurance that a 609 will remove an item in your credit report even with the full backing of the law. As such, you should never pay for a single 609 template or even hire a professional to draft the letter for you.

That being said, there is nothing wrong with exercising your rights as a citizen and consumer. If you are diligent in monitoring your reports and can back up your claims, you can remove errors from your entry which would fix your credit score.

And if the alleged errors are verified to be true and accurate, you can rest that such negative remarks won't stay in your report forever. At best, they will affect your score for a good 7 years or so.

This will give you plenty of time to build some habits that will naturally tend toward improving your overall credit score.

Chapter IX: The Basics of Debt Management

We have talked previously about how debt is inescapable for most people. As such, your ability to pay off your debts is going to be crucial to improve your credit score.

Here's the problem, however: most people don't have a plan when it comes to paying their debt. What you have to remember is that you also have to spend a bit to live while you are actively cutting down on the size of your financial obligations.

Luckily for you, dealing with your debt is not as complicated as might think. It will involve a process that, consequently, requires you to come up with a plan. To do so, here are a few things to consider first.

Why Your Debt isn't Decreasing

Before anything else, you must understand why you are not able to cut your debt down to a smaller size. This has got to be the most frustrating aspect of being in debt as none of your actions seem to take out huge parts of your existing balance. There are four plausible reasons for this.

1. **Interest**

Remember that your monthly payments will cover a portion of the principal amount you borrowed plus the interest. If you are focusing more on paying the interest, you are not taking a huge part of the principal amount.

Here's an example. Supposed that you owe a creditor $200.00 who imposes to you a $5.00 monthly fee plus 5% interest. This means that you should be paying at least $5.00 every month plus interest of 10% for a total of $15.00.

Sounds reasonable, right? If you think about it, you are chipping away a mere 0.75% of your total debt every month.

In practice, a portion of what you are paying is not going to cutting down your balance. Instead, it goes directly to the lender's pocket so they earn from "investing" in you.

If you keep at that rate, you'd be stuck paying your debt for a good 12 to 13 months. And that's just for small loans. What about the huge housing and car loans that take decades to complete? You'd be losing a sizeable portion of your income paying something that does not necessarily go into cutting down the size of your debt.

2. **Penalties**

Just like with interest, the penalties you incur impede your ability to cut down on your outstanding balance. Every financial contract you sign up for comes with some penalties if you fail to pay your dues on time.

So, going back to the $200.00 example above, what if the lender imposes an additional $5.00 penalty if you pay a day late? You would have to fork out $20.00 of your cash to pay your creditor and only 50% of that amount is going to reduce your balance.

Of course, the easiest way to avoid penalties is to uphold your end of the bargain. Just pay your dues on time and in the method that you and your creditor agreed to.

Another way you could avoid penalties is to look at the contract you are about to sign up for. If you don't like the terms, you can avoid incurring them by negotiating for a more favorable payment scheme.

For credit card holders, there are additional penalties if you tend to max out on your balance frequently. You can avoid such penalties by keeping your spending within your monthly limit.

3. **New Debt**

If you have undergone a debt cycle, this one will be quite familiar for you. This usually occurs when you create new debt while you are still trying to pay your current accounts.

Here's an example. Let us say that have a loan worth $5,000.00 and have already paid $2,500.00 of it. However, for some reason, you loaned another $2,000.00 from a different creditor.

So, instead of your total debt going down by 50%, you added another 40% to it, putting your total debt at $4,500.00. Since this is another creditor, you will also have to deal with compound interest so more of your money will go into paying your interests aside from the total balance.

The best solution for this? Just don't borrow money while you are still paying off your debts. Of course, some strategies will require you to open a new account but this is more for consolidating your debt to easily manage your accounts.

4. **Sticking by the Minimum**

Sticking by what the contract tells you is noble. It just gives your lender the impression that you are upholding your end of the bargain.

However, by sticking to the minimum amount, you are prolonging the effects your debt has on your credit score. If you have agreed to pay a $5,000.00 loan in 3 years in installments plus a 10% interest rate, that means you'd have to deal with the obligation for a good 36 months or so.

That also means that you allow your lender to profit from you for a good 3 years until you paid your balance in full.

Of course, your only solution here is to pay more than what is the minimum every month.

Dealing with Debt

Whatever reason there is to why your debt is not getting any smaller, you would agree that effective debt management requires speed and precision on your part. Thus, your debt management strategy should focus on finding a way to take out huge chunks of your balance while softening the blow from penalties, interests, and other surcharges.

This is where having a plan will become quite important. Your plan need not be elaborate or long. All you have to do to have a semblance of a plan is to answer three questions:

1. **What Strategy works for me?**
2. **How can I reduce interests and penalties while dealing with the principal amount?**
3. **What should I not do when I am still dealing with my debts?**

Step 1: Debt Reduction

The core goal in this phase is to pay more so you won't have to deal with your debts for longer. So, how do you go about doing that? There are two strategies that you can use here.

A. **The Snowball Method**

This strategy is quite simple yet effective in building the "momentum" needed to take off a consistent amount of accounts from your entire list of debts.

As the name would imply, this strategy requires you to start small and work your way to the top. You can do this by listing all the debts that you have in ascending order.

For example, you have 5 credit cards. Your balances for each card are as follows: $1,000.00 for Card A, $2,500.00 for Card B, $500.00 for Card C, $5,000.00 for Card D, and $1,500.00 for Card E.

All you have to do then is to arrange them according to their balance size from smallest to largest. So your list of priority would look like this:

1. **Card C - $ 500.00**
2. **Card A - $1,000.00**
3. **Card E - $1,500.00**
4. **Card B - $2,500.00**
5. **Card D – $5,000.00**

It does not matter how long you have to pay for each respective loan so as long as you get to clear items off your list faster. With time and consistency on your part, you might just clear off all your debts one at a time.

Aside from debt management, this strategy is good for promoting better financial habits. By forcing yourself to focus more on clearing your debt list, you become more cautious with how you spend your monthly earnings. As such, you should become less impulsive with your spending which should prevent you from incurring more debt.

A. The Avalanche Method

This strategy is the complete inverse of the snowball method as it focuses on the biggest amounts in your debt list first. As such, you will be arranging your debts in descending order. If we use the same example above, your debt list could look like this.

1. Card D - $5,000.00
2. Card B - $2,500.00
3. Card E - $1,500.00
4. Card A - $1,000.00
5. Card C - $ 500.00

One major drawback to this strategy is that it takes a while for you to clear off items from your list. However, what it does is that it takes huge chunks of your cumulative debt more consistently.

In the example above, your total debt is at $10,500.00. By paying the $5,000.00 first, you are effectively removing approximately 48% of your total debt.

At the same time, you have to consider the interest rates. Remember that interest rates are ancillary fees. They only exist for as long as the principal obligation is there. If you can take out that loan as quickly as possible, a portion of your cumulative interest gets removed.

Important: Debt size is not the only factor that you can use when prioritizing which debts to clear first. You can use APRs when organizing your list like ordering your debts from the smallest APRs to the largest. You can also use contract duration like prioritizing the debts that take a few years to finish over the ones that cover a decade or more.

Which of these Strategies Will Work?

If we are honest about it, both strategies are viable options for anyone. The Snowball is recommended for those with multiple short-term loans while the Avalanche might work best for those with a few long-term loans.

However, they only work to your benefit if you can:

● Increase your monthly income
● Decrease your monthly spending

- Avoid incurring new debt

Step 2: Attacking the Interest

Always remember that your debt management plan is not going to be done within a few weeks. Depending on how much you owe, this could take a month and a few to successfully pull off or years.

And while you are dealing with the principal amount, you'd have to deal with the interest. There is a way to soften the blow of these rates and the strategies below might just help you.

A. Zero Interest Cards

There are some credit cards out there that allow you to pay off your debts without having to deal with an interest rate. Such a 0% interest grace period could last for a year or two depending on the terms of the card provider.

Using these cards, then, means that you can pay more of the principal amount for a good 12 to 24 months.

Use this to your advantage by making sure that a huge portion of the debt gets removed within that period.

We'll talk about this option in detail when get to talking about credit card interest (which is coincidentally the next chapter). However, what you need to know now is that this card, if offered to you, is something that you should consider taking as soon as possible.

2. **Debt Consolidation**

There are programs out there that allow you to consolidate your debt into one account. How this works is rather simple: a lender would loan you a considerable amount of money which you would then use to pay off every single debt that you have.

For example, you have 5 creditors which you owe $500.00, $1,000.00, $2,000.00, $3,500.00, and $4,000.00 respectively. To get the money to pay off your debt, you would apply for a consolidation program which would then loan to you an amount equal to your total debt.

For this case, that loan would be $11,000.00. Now, all you have to do to then would be to pay off every single creditor on your list.

What makes consolidation effective is that you are putting all your financial obligations into one account which makes it easier for you to manage. Also, because you have paid all your debts from your previous creditors, all interest rates have ceased to exist.

So, instead of 5 creditors with 5 different interest rates, you now have to deal with 1 creditor with 1 interest rate. Also, consolidation loans tend to have interest rates that are comparatively lower than more conventional loans. That low rate remains the same for the entire duration of the contract.

Of course, there are potential problems to deal with when you consolidate your loan. First, payment terms will be stricter for you. Failing to pay the minimum amount will cause your score to drop by the hundreds.

Next, the amount that you have to pay plus interest will be larger than your previous monthly fees combined. This is because you are now dealing with a larger loan.

Lastly, this strategy does not consider the probability of you racking up more debt to pay off your consolidation loan. If you do incur more debt from other creditors while you are still in debt consolidation, you are effectively making things harder for yourself.

3. **Non-Card Alternatives**

You can also avail of other funding options like peer-to-peer loans, digital loaning services, and programs from savings societies. What makes them viable options is that they don't require security or have more lenient background checks.

The time it takes for your loan to get approved is also quicker. In some digital platforms, that process could take mere seconds to finish. The only drawback is that these people can still report you to the CRAs if you don't pay them. Also, some of these loaning programs tend to veer towards predatory practices.

Step 3: Avoiding Some Mistakes

As you might have noticed, much of your debt management efforts are utterly dependent on your choices as a credit holder. In this phase, there are two things that you must never perform:

A. **Not Changing Your Spending Habits**

At this point, you should adjust your spending since you have creditors to deal with. But how could you subsist every month if your money goes into paying debts?

For starters, you have to know how to spend your money wisely. Things like food and your utilities are always a necessity so never skimp on those expenses. But for non-essential expenses like out-of-town trips and regular restaurant dinners, can be avoided until you clear off your debt list.

So, you are limiting your spending per se but only to the more frivolous ones.

That way, more of your money can be used to pay your dues. Living like your creditors are not after you is not ideal at this point.

B. **Not Communicating with Your Creditors**

The worst thing that you can do to your creditor is cutting off all forms of communication with them. This includes avoiding their calls or not answering them when they come knocking at your door.

Just remember that these people can easily influence your credit report. All it takes is for them to send a negative remark to the reporting agency and your score will drop by several points. And let us not forget the more ruthless, predatory creditors who will not hesitate to threaten, harm, and humiliate you just to make you pay up.

Instead of pretending that these creditors don't exist, try to maintain an open line of communication. You have to let them know that you are trying to pay all your debts and that you have not forgotten your obligation to them.

Sure, some creditors will not be as understanding as others but you should impress to them that you have no intention of bailing out on your debts.

At most, you give yourself enough space to renegotiate your payment terms or ask them to hold off on reporting you until you start paying. There's no assurance that they will agree to such terms but there is no harm in trying.

Will Consolidating Your Debt

Improve Your Credit Score?

In a manner of speaking, yes. What you have to remember is that debt consolidation programs, by nature, favor credit recovery efforts to a certain degree.

How this works is rather simple: You have to remember that creditors mark every payment you make to debt as a positive entry on your credit report. So, as you are paying your initial debts, every payment and complete fulfillment of your obligations will be noted.

And even if you have a new account opened, every payment you make on that consolidation account will also be marked as a positive entry in your report. In essence, you are allowed to stack up on positive entries in your report with one consolidation account. At best, this allows your score to enter into the 600 to 700 FICO range once your consolidation loan has been fully paid.

Before Your Consolidate....

Like every other debt management strategy out there, consolidation will only work under specific conditions. Before you consider this option, here are a few things to consider.

1. **Do Keep Payments Timely**

As was previously stated, your ability to pay your monthly fees will matter more when consolidating your debt. Missing one payment is going to hurt your credit score more than missing payments on standard loans.

2. **Your Other Repair Strategies**

Debt consolidation might be effective but whatever you do outside of this strategy will also affect your credit score. Always remember that credit utilization and history heavily impact your score. As such, a healthy balance between used and available credit as well as a long history of good payments will keep your score up.

What happens, then, if you close a card with a lot of available credit and with years' worth of timely payments? Your credit utilization ratio would shift which can cause your score to drop.

If that card has been with you for 5 years at least, closing that card will erase 5 years from your history. In turn, this causes your credit score to drop.

The point is that your other credit repair strategies must coincide with your consolidation plan. If their goals run contrary to each other, they would ultimately cancel each other's benefits.

3. **Your Patience**

Debt consolidation is a rather slow and arduous strategy. You can expect little to no changes in your next credit report if you use strategy.

What consolidation and management are good at is stacking up on every minor achievement you make over a period spanning several years. It takes a while for you to see massive changes in your score but the benefits that this strategy will offer will last for quite a while.

If you do follow the plan and clear off a lot of items in your debt list, your score should go beyond the 600-point mark in a few years. This is provided, of course, that you don't incur any other major financial obligation for the duration of the plan.

Chapter X: Dealing with Interest

When you are in debt, you will find out that your monthly payments towards that obligation involve more than what you owe to your creditor. And if you do agree to pay in installments, you will notice that the total amount that you will pay for your loan would be more than what you borrowed.

This is simply what is called Interest. And for many credit holders, this the part of their obligation that they fail to fully comprehend. Interest plays a crucial role in your ability to handle your debt and, in turn, would affect your credit score. Thus, learning how it works is necessary to improve your rating at the reporting agencies.

What is Interest?

To start things off, the proper term for Interest in the context of debt is your Annual Percentage Rate. Every person gets their own APR which the creditor determines by considering several factors. One of these factors happens to be your credit score.

The general rule is that the APR you will get is inversely proportional to the quality of your credit score. The higher your credit score gets, the lower your APR will be upon applying for a credit card.

Credit card companies use your APR to determine how much they are going to charge you daily. The formula varies from lender to lender but the easiest version of it is this:

Daily Interest = (APR/100)/365 Days

So, for example, if your creditor gave you an APR of 5% which you will then divide by 100 which gives you the number of 0.05. You then divide this by the number of days in that year which would yield you the figure of 0.00013%. This is your daily interest rate which will be added to your remaining balance at the end of that day.

This is a process called Compounding Interest which occurs every 30 days. Let us say that your credit card has an available balance of $5,000.00 and your current daily interest rate is 0.00013%.

By multiplying your available balance with your interest rate, you will get an amount of $0.65. This will be the daily interest you will be charged with. Multiply that number by 30 and you will get $19.50 which will be the monthly interest you will be charged with.

The Big Problem

"So It's a few extra bucks...." You say to yourself. "Where is the problem?"

The answer lies in the duration of your obligation. For short-term loans, interest is rarely an inconvenience. But for large loans that take years to complete, you can notice how much of your money will be going to the payment of your interest.

Let us go back to the example above. What if you must pay for your loan on an installment basis for 3 years? This means that you have 36 monthly payments of $138.88 plus interest of

$19.50. In a span of 3 years, you spent approximately $700.00 on interest alone which is 14% of the money you borrowed from that creditor.

That could have gone to your savings account to help you later on. And what if, aside from this creditor, you also have other creditors along with your monthly expenses? Much of your income would be spent every month and none of it would go into preparing for your future.

Credit Grace Periods

Here's a secret that many creditors would not want to share with you: interest is not always automatically applied to your account. For credit card companies, there is the chance that you will be given a "grace period" of sorts where you will pay only the monthly fee.

That period's duration can be dependent on your agreement but lenient creditors can have this period go for a few months or half a year.

Here is the catch, however: you need to either be in the good graces of the creditor or make a good impression by way of your credit score to be allowed this grace period.

Also, you forfeit such a grace period if you start missing payments in the first few months of the contract. To know if you can avail of this grace period, just check the terms on your agreement before signing it.

0% Interest Cards

The previous chapter introduced you to the concept of a zero percent interest card. In most cases, this card can help you manage your debt as more of your money can be used to taking off huge chunks of the principal amount instead of going to the APR fee.

Due to their unique characteristics, a lot of credit holders do not know how to use them properly. Here are some facts that you need to about these cards so you can take advantage of every feature that they offer.

1. Applicability

Sad to say, 0% interest cards have yet to be made for general application. Sure, the card provider might advertise it as offering 0% APR but what they are not telling you is that they might be referring to something else.

If you want to know where the 0% is going to be applied, look at the rates included in the offer. APR can be applied in several aspects like:

A. Purchases

As the name would imply, the 0% interest would be applied when you use your card to buy something. If you are dependent on your credit card for your transactions, you better make sure that the interest applies here to make paying for your purchases easier later on.

Also, the 0% APR for purchases can be lumped with balance transfers. If it is, just remember that these two features might have different duration periods.

B. Balance Transfers

When you want your accounts to move to another card, this will help you by paying only for the transfer fee. If you are going to consolidate all your debts, this is the feature you should make certain is included in your card. Otherwise, you still have to pay for the interest in your balances while transferring them to your new card.

C. **Cash Advances**

This will apply only for transactions that require a downpayment for a service or valuable real property like homes and vehicles. Out of all the 0% features, this is perhaps the rarest as not a lot of card providers would offer it to any credit holder, even those with good scores.

D. **Penalties**

Penalty rates are present if you fail to meet certain conditions with your credit card providers. In this instance, a 0% interest rate will not help you. Any benefit that the 0% interest might offer is going to be countered by the effects of that penalty.

2. **The 0% Interest Feature CAN be Terminated**

Always remember that your 0% interest card is still a credit card. This means that you will have to abide by certain conditions to take full advantage of its features. The most common requirement is that you regularly pay off your balance on a set date.

If the payment is due and you are late by even a day, the credit card provider will issue you a warning that your 0% interest feature is in danger of being canceled. If they are strict, they can cancel the deal either in the second instance you fail to pay or, worse, if you cannot provide an ample explanation why you missed your payment.

The credit card provider can also automatically report your missing payment to the CRAs. As such, failing to meet the requirements of your 0% interest card will not only cause the cancellation of your agreement with the creditor but also a massive drop in your score.

3. Credit Utilization still Matters

Since this is still a credit card, the 0% interest card still abides by the same rules, especially with credit utilization. As such, you should remain within the 30% threshold when using your new card.

If you secured that card to use for a big purchase, you can expect your utilization to jump up and affect your credit score. And if you do max out, just make that a motivation of sorts for you to clear that debt as quickly as you can.

4. **0% Does Not Last Forever**

Remember those credit "grace periods" mentioned in the last few paragraphs? The 0% interest rate works in the same manner and for the same duration as well.

This is because the 0% feature is for purely promotional purposes. It is there to draw potential credit holders in so that the provider can profit from the subscriptions that they could receive.

Once the period ends, you can expect the regular APR to be put in effect. If you still have remaining balances when that period ends, you can expect your interest rate to start negatively affecting your score until you pay off that debt.

As such, always be mindful when you start using that card. The 0% interest period can last between 12 months to 24 months. Use that time to your advantage and pay off large portions of the principal amount that you owe.

5. **It's a Limited Offer**

Aside from the 12-24 month limit for the 0% interest rate, the card itself is in short supply for every lender. This is why a credit card provider will be stricter to 0% interest cardholders as they are expected to be a bit more mindful with how they use their card compared to regular cardholders.

Of course, some lenders might offer you multiple cards aside from the 0% card. This is most likely to set a limit on your total account balance and encourage you to pay off your debt as quickly as possible.

So if you want to transfer your balance to a 0% interest card, you'd have to meet the lender's strict requirements. This will include preparing the necessary paperwork and, of course, possessing a credit score no lower than 600.

6. **There will be Transfer Limits**

Even if you do get approved for a balance transfer, there is no assurance that the lender will approve of the amount of debt that you want to be transferred to that card.

For example, let us say that you want to transfer $15,000.00 worth in debt to a 0% interest card. Even if you have a good credit score and you met all the lender's requirements, there is a strong chance that the amount to be transferred will be $10,000.00 at best or $5,000.00.

This goes back to the lender's level of trust in you as well as their prerogative. It is up to them to allow a full or partial transfer. And when the latter happens, you will have to figure out for yourself what to do with the remaining un-transferred amount.

7. **It is not Always Useful**

What if you are the person that can pay all your debts in full every month? A 0% interest card will not offer a lot to you since there is no balance in your cards. Therefore, there is no interest to deal with in the first place.

A 0% interest card is ideal for those people that intend to make huge purchases with payment terms that go beyond 6 months. It could also be geared towards credit holders who want to improve make adjustments on their spending habits to improve on an already good credit score.

Reducing Interest

Since interest will take up a considerable portion of what you have to pay every month for your debts, then it makes that you have to find a way to deal with less of it. Is that possible? The answer is yes.

There are some simple yet important habits and strategies that you can apply to soften the blow of interest in your monthly payments.

1. **Paying More than the Minimum**

Let us say that you owe $4,000.00 to your creditor with a 15% interest. The creditor requires you to make a minimum payment of $20.00 every month. This means that it will take you no less than 200 months to clear off the entire balance. That's 200 months of paying $20.00 for the principal and the 15% interest.

What if you paid $100.00 every month, then? That's only 40 months or 3 years and 4 months of dealing with the interest. Increase that amount further to $200.00 and you'd deal with the interest for only 20 months or 1 year and 8 months. The point is that you are going to deal with debt and interest less the more you pay to clear off the principal amount.

This is assuming, of course, that you have enough money to spare every month to pay off your debts.

2. **Negotiate for a Lower Rate**

Here's another secret that you need to know now: Your interest is not final. No law requires creditors to impose an interest which means that there is an industry standard for calculating how much lenders can impose in interest on borrowers.

What this also means is that you can negotiate for a more reasonable payment term. Call your creditor and see if you can negotiate a new interest rate. Explain to them why you are having a hard time dealing with the current interest rate, what you can manage to earn every month, and what other payments you have to make.

Of course, you have to be open to the idea that the creditor will reject your proposal. If they do, just make your payments and then call again in the future. Perhaps they are more willing to negotiate when their mood is better and they could see that you are faithfully upholding your end of the bargain.

3. **Time Your Payments Right**

There are some creditors out there who only impose interest on short-term loans if you fail to pay your debt on the due date. And unless a specific time deadline was set for that day, you have the entire full working day (8 AM to 5 PM) to pay your debt.

And this does give rise to the question: is interest automatically added to your balance if you pay late? Not exactly.

The counting for the period of adding the Interest rate starts from the day you applied for that loan or made a purchase until the date that the first payment becomes due. However, there is a small delay of a few hours or a day before the creditor imposes the interest as they have to prepare a new statement to be sent to your address.

Thus, you have a small window of opportunity to pay for the balance until the Interest is added. And if the Interest and penalty are still reflected on your next bill or the balance is still reflected on your next credit report, you can always file a dispute and request for an amendment.

To Conclude

What you will have to remember is that Interest is an ancillary charge. This means that it exists so as long as the principal obligation does.

As such, your strategy in dealing with Interest should not only focus on reducing its size but also the duration of the entire obligation. By paying more of the principal amount every month until the balance is paid in full, you won't have to deal with whatever interest rate that was imposed on you for longer than necessary.

Chapter XI: Credit Boosting and Other Lifestyle Changes

At this point, you should have understood that your ability to handle your debt will play a crucial role in improving your score. However, that is not all there is to a sound credit repair strategy. There are also some minor adjustments that you can make in your lifestyle that can help in improving your score by several points.

Financial Linking

There are many entries in your credit report that you can dispute. However, the people that you are financially linked to are a bit hard to dispute.

Financial links are simply the relationships that the credit reporting agencies think that you may have with another person. These are no mere relationships where you are associated with another person. When there is a financial link, there is also the existence of joint liability between two persons.

To be deemed financially linked to another person, you must either:

A. Open a joint account with them.
B. Apply for joint credit.
C. Be a guarantor for somebody else applying for a loan.
D. Receive a judgment in a civil collection case where you are deemed jointly and solidarily liable with another person in regards to debt.

As to where you will find these financial links, just look at the Payment History section of your credit report. The lender will note any transaction you have made with another person in the data that they submitted to the agency. Any person that was named in that entry will be marked as your Financial Associate.

Also, you could look at the Public Documents section for any court-related financial link. Some CRAs also relegate all financial links in a separate section so it is easier for you to trace them in the report.

Do Financial Links affect your Credit Score?

The answer is no. Your credit score is going to be tabulated based on your actions alone. It would be unfair on your part to get a poor score because someone you know made some poor financial decisions.

However, they do negatively affect your impression with creditors. Even if you have a good credit score, lenders might hesitate in approving your loan if such a loan was jointly made with a person whose rating is not as good as yours.

The nature of your accounts would also matter here. If that person has access to your account since it was jointly made with them, what's stopping them from using the credits there and leaving both of you with a large debt? If the account was jointly made, the way your associate handles their money will indirectly affect the impression creditors have on you.

However, being associated with someone having a good credit score will surprisingly help you. The only condition is that you are new to the concept of handling credit and have no previous demerits.

Disputing Links

Since financial associations count as an entry, you are entitled to dispute their inclusion in your report. For example, if a person made a transaction with the joint creditor but did not notify you of such, you can inform the credit reporting agency of such. The agency is then required to verify the information and make the necessary amendments.

Also, you can propose an opt-out agreement with your creditor. This is where you can compel the creditor to remove any transaction made by a financial associate of yours if you can notify them that such an action was not made with your consent. This way, the transaction by your associate would not be reflected in your credit report.

Buying Now, Paying Later

One of the major adjustments that we have made since the outbreak of COVID-19 is in our buying habits. Since we cannot go out of our houses as easily compared to a few years ago, there has been an increase in online purchases since 2020.

A lot of these online marketplaces work with a "Buy Now, Pay Later" (BNPL) scheme where you can order what you want and then have to pay for it at a later date.

So, does BNPL hurt your credit score? The answer is no.

At least not directly.

Usually, when you try to buy anything, your purchasing power is going to be limited by the amount of money you have on hand or in your bank account. In short, if you don't have the money to pay for something at any given time, you can't buy it.

The BNPL scheme, however, flips that script as you can buy now for whatever you want and have to deal with the financial obligations later.

By removing the guilt that usually comes when making an impulsive purchase decision while still allowing a person to feel that rush from the buying process, BNPL systems can increase one's tendency to overspend.

At its very worst, being exposed to a BNPL scheme can lead to an increase in missed payments, poor budgeting skills, and debt. And these factors, in turn, would heavily affect your credit score.

That does not mean that online shopping platforms are not aware of how much their systems encourage people to be reckless with their spending. For starters, they impose daily limits or prevent a person from purchasing another item until they have settled their outstanding balances.

Also, these online shops can still report erring buyers to their credit reporting agencies for every missed payment. At the very least, some safety nets can prevent you from incurring a lot of debt within these platforms.

Thus, the same rule still applies in online shopping: Never live above your means. Base your purchasing decisions on necessity and availability of funds. If that item is something that you need and can pay for with the available cash in your wallet, then do so. If it neither important nor payable with your current available money, then hold off on that purchase until you are in better financial standing.

Credit Builder Cards

A credit builder card is a financial product that you can use to increase your score so that it reaches the 650-800 range in a few months.

When you are issued a credit builder card, that card will initially be useless. To activate its basic functions, you will have to pay a deposit either in increments or a one-time payment. This will act as a security for your card while also giving the lender the impression that can be trusted when it comes to handling money.

As such, a credit builder card is ideal for people who want to build on their credit while also enjoying the ability to qualify for loans. A credit builder card is recommended if you:

A. Are relatively new to the concept of handling credit.
B. Had issues with debt management in the past.
C. Had a business that previously went bankrupt.
D. Were compelled to pay your debt in a collection suit at court.

Pros and Cons

A credit builder card can benefit you in two ways. First, it can build on your reputation with creditors. The way it does is through the payments you made to "activate" the credit builder feature of the card. Each deposit will be a positive remark which the lender will then report to the CRAs.

In a month or so and depending on the size of your downpayment, you can expect your credit score to go up by 100-200 points in your next credit report. There is no assurance that your score can reach the 700-800 range but at least it can reach 600 which is good enough for some basic loans.

The next benefit is more on habit formation. By compelling you to pay for its most basic features, the card helps you prioritize paying for your obligations over enjoying the benefits of the card. If you are serious about building your credit, the card will help you become more disciplined with your spending habits once the features of the card are activated.

However, there are some issues that you have to deal with if you choose to use this card. First, the interest rate is rather high. Remember that a credit builder card is not easily issued to anyone. The creditor will have to test your reliability which is why they will pose such a high-interest rate. On paper, this is meant to encourage you to be as consistent as possible with your monthly payments.

Next, these cards have rather low credit limits. At best, you can expect the limits here to go no further than $5,000.00. This is because a credit builder card is a credit boosting product first and a credit card second.

Fortunately for you, these limitations are only there in the first few months. With constant payments, you might qualify for a reduced rate and an increase in credit limit.

Making Payments Matter

One cursory glance at your credit score would tell you that not all of your transactions are going to be reported. This might harm you in the long term as some of the regular payments you make can give the impression that you know how to manage your financial obligations. It is only that they are not being included in the data being sent to the CRAs.

The agencies, Experian in particular, are finding ways to correct this discrepancy. As of now, Experian offers two services to increase the visibility of your payments in your credit score.

A. **Boost**

Experian's Boost program was designed to highlight one of the payments you regularly make but is rarely considered on your credit report: Utilities.

The premise is rather simple with this program. Anybody can choose to skip on paying credit and luxury investments. For something so basic yet crucial to living like electricity, water, Internet access, and gas? Those are some services that no person can live without for a month.

This is why Boost was designed to make the payments you regularly make to utility companies all the more visible in your credit report. By adding these payments to your list of positive transactions, your score is expected to go up by a few points.

Also, Boost is designed to monitor every payment you make to your utility companies by way of your bank account. This has the bonus of increasing your credit history which should boost your score even further.

Using Boost

To qualify for the Boost service, you must have an account with Experian first. You will need to fill in the basic information sheet as well as provide information in areas such as:

- **Mode of Payment -** Boost will monitor every payment you make through your bank account. As such, have your method of payment for your utilities be set at a Bank Payment first.

- **Payment History -** You should have made at least 3 separate and consecutive monthly payments to your utility company through the bank account of your choice. Boost's search bots need to establish your consistency in paying your bills before they start including your utility payments in your report.

- **Utilities -** Every service and utility you subscribe to must be included and in their separate accounts. Boost does not mark compound bills or any payment you make by way of a proxy.

- **Credit Account -** You must include at least one credit account in your Boost profile. This is to identify you as a legitimate credit card user.

Once you have set your profile, the service will start monitoring every utility payment you make. You will know that they will be included as new entries will be made in your next credit report.

B. CreditLadder

Like Boost, Experian's CreditLadder program also aims to highlight another payment you regularly make: Rent. Again the core premise of this service lies in the fact that paying rent tends to be one of your topmost priorities every month.

If you have to choose between paying off a creditor who is far away from you and your landlord who is closer and can immediately penalize you, you'd prioritize the latter. This way, you still have a place to live and sleep in for the next month while you find ways to pay off your other creditors.

How CreditLadder works will also quite simple. If you successfully applied for their service, the program will go through your personal information to look for every payment like where you live and the identity of your landlord. Once this is determined, the program will then look for any entry indicating that you have been regularly paying your rental fees.

Of course, this data will then be sent to Experian's data banks as well as Equifax. You will know that your rental payments have been included since they will pop up in your next credit report.

What About Your Landlord?

Since this service covers your rental payments, does Credit Ladder require the consent of your landlord first? Technically, no.

Instead, what Credit Ladder does is contact your landlord to confirm the information that they discovered in your files. They will require the specifics of your agreement as well as your chosen method of payment. These are information that only your landlord can independently confirm.

Once confirmed, your payments will then be submitted for inclusion in your credit report. So as long as a pattern of consistent payments is established, you could expect your score to go up by several points.

Important Note: If you are considering subscribing to Boost and Credit Ladder, do keep in mind that these services are designed to cater to credit holders with little to no credit history at all. If you have a long history of good and consistent payments to your creditors, there is not much that these services can offer you. At best, they can make your already-good score slightly better.

Protecting Your Credit Information

Fraud is perhaps one of the most pervasive and relentless problems in the world of Finance. You would be surprised how many credit holders out there do not properly protect their information which results in it being stolen and used for a lot of credit-score-ruining actions.

So as long as these unauthorized are not verified to be done without your permission, they will remain as negative remarks on your score. As such, your best option is to prevent unwanted incursions to your score.

Here's how:

A. **Keep a Low Profile**

You must be able to cover your tracks so that attackers have a limited angle to which they could attack you. The simplest thing that you can do is to log in to your accounts on a few selected devices. For example, you will only use your laptop for online transactions and your mobile device for social media. By locking in your transactions into one device, you can narrow down where you are most likely going to be the most vulnerable.

It is also necessary that you be mindful as to what you share online and on what platform. A major mistake many first-time credit holders make is to brag about their new cards which expose the numbers embedded therein. In short, you are goading online predators to take a shot at you.

B. **Know a Fraud When You See One**

Like predatory credit practices, you have to know when somebody online is setting you up for a fraud attempt. For instance, you might receive an email from your "bank" that your card has just been terminated and they need confirmation of your information.

Before you click on the link, you have to identify if the link itself leads to your bank's official website. You can easily tell since banks do advertise their official sites and are simple enough to read. For example, JP Morgan Chase's official website is www.jpmorganchase.com.

One other phishing attempt you have to be careful of is any offer for freebies in exchange for your private information. Think about it, do you know of any person that is kind enough to give millions of dollars to a stranger over the internet?

Again, you must apply the rule: if the offer is too good to be true, it usually is.

C. **Improve on Your Security**

Aside from your vigilance, your devices must have the most up-to-date security that can thwart off cyber-attacks. The easiest thing that you can do here is to improve your password combinations. It must be something that is hard to figure out and contains a mix of letters, numbers, and symbols.

You should also be mindful of where you store your cards. Keep track of which ones you are currently using especially if you go out. This way, they won't figure in transactions that you most definitely did not authorize.

Conclusion: Sustaining Improvements

The bulk of your credit repair efforts will focus on making your score reach the 600-point mark. After all, this is the point when your credit score will no longer serve as a detriment to any transaction that you would want to take part in.

And what happens, then, if you do repair your score? What if you not only reached the 600-point mark but managed to reach the 700 to 800 scores?

The obvious answer is to sustain the changes that you have made to your score. Do not get the wrong idea, though. It is impossible to maintain the same numerical score for the next consecutive reports due to FICO's complex formula.

Instead, your next best option is to keep it within a specific range. To do this, there are several things that you must consider.

Establishing a Strong Payment History

The most direct option you could take is to simply stack up on positive remarks from your creditors by way of making constant payments. When it comes to your payment history, there are only three things that you have to remember:

A. Pay On-Time

It does not matter how large of a timetable you have set to settle your debts. You should be able to monitor when your payments are due and prepare enough money to pay for them.

It is recommended that you pay your dues before the date.

B. Pay More

The minimum monthly fee is exactly just that, the minimum. Going beyond that minimum is what will help you clear off large portions of your debt while also minimizing the length of your exposure towards interest rates.

C. **Pay Often**

A constant rate of payment for your balances is the only way you could chip away at your debt until it is gone. If you combine this with an ability to pay for more than the minimum, you could effectively clear off items in your debt list at a faster rate.

Report Monitoring

You have to remember that a report is only final when you don't dispute it. This means that you have to be as meticulous as possible when reviewing your report.

Check that every item there is 100% true and accurate. Be extra mindful when it comes to wrongly attributed data, missing or recurring entries, and unauthorized transactions.

And when you do find them, you can always dispute the report at the agency preparing it. This is also why you must keep a record of all the contracts you sign as well as receipts for every transaction you make with your cards. This way, you would have evidence to back up your claims.

And do not worry about regularly disputing the accuracy of your report. Consumer protection laws require credit reporting agencies to provide credit holders with an accurate and factual account of all their transactions for a certain period.

Lastly, always remember this tip when disputing your score: Go beyond your score. Though important, your credit score is only a numerical representation of your credit standing. It is at the details of your report where you can find discrepancies that you can dispute.

Discipline

Perhaps the most important change you can make is in your habits. When it comes to your credit, you must be able to optimize the usage of your available finances. This will involve prioritizing where you spend your money as well as finding new sources of income.

Of course, you must be able to get yourself out of debt quickly. There's no denying that debt is often unavoidable. You can even incur new debt while you are dealing with current ones, depending on your situation. However, a sound debt management plan (and having some emergency funding) can spell the difference between you clearing off your obligations or getting overwhelmed by them.

To Conclude

Building your credit score is not exactly straightforward but it is not that complicated either. It will involve a series of changes in the way you live, spend your money, and manage your financial obligations.

But once you do improve your standing with creditors, all that is left to do is to protect that score while also building on your success. There is no doubt that the road to recovery for your credit score is going to be demanding but the rewards you can enjoy do last.

Thank you for taking the time to read this book. I hope that you have learned quite a lot and now know what you need to do to improve your credit score. All that is left to do now is to apply all that you have learned out there.

Good Luck!

Resources

Books

1. Graham, W.R., "Credits Repair Secrets: Learn the Strategies and Techniques of Consultants and Credit Attorneys to Fix your Bad Debt and Improve your Business or Personal Finance. Including Dispute Letters" Amazon, 2021.

2. Johnson, A. "The Ultimate Credit Repair Guide to Having Luxurious Credit, Amazon, 2016.

3. Weaver, B. "The Easy Section 609 Credit Repair Secret: Remove All Negative Accounts In 30 Days Using A Federal Law Loophole That Works Every Time", 2017.

4. Bucci, S. "Credit Repair Kit for Dummies", 2014.

5. Stone, S. "The Credit Building Manual: The Most Effective Beginner Friendly Manual That Will Build Your Credit and Raise Your Credit Score Quickly and Efficiently". 2020.

6. Adams, O. "Fix Your Credit Transform Your Life", 2021.3.30

7. Croix, M. "The DebtClear Roadmap: A Hacker's Guide to Debt Relief, Credit Repair, Asset Protection, and Creditor Lawsuits", 2011.

8. Ramsey, D. "The Total Money Makeover: Classic Edition: A Proven Plan for Financial Fitness", 2013.

Journals

1. Agarwal, S., Ambrose, B.W., and Liu, C., "Credit Lines and Credit Utilization", Journal of Money, Credit, and Banking, 0.1353/mcb.2006.0010, 2006.

2. Lee, C.W.,Kuo, C.K., "Examining the Validity of Credit Ratings Assigned to Credit Derivatives", Global Credit Review, 10.1142/s201049361550004x, 2015.

Website Articles

1. Majaski, C. "Default vs. Delinquency: What's the Difference?", Investopedia, April 14, 2019.

Link:https://www.investopedia.com/ask/answers/062315/what-are-differences-between-delinquency-and-default.asp

2. Paperno, B. "7 Common Myths About How Bankruptcy Affects Credit", MarketWatch, March 16, 2018. Link: https://www.marketwatch.com/story/7-common-myths-about-how-bankruptcy-affects-credit-2018-03-16

3. Crail, C. "5 Ways to Protect Your Credit in 2021", Forbes, January 11, 2021.
Link:https://www.forbes.com/advisor/credit-cards/ways-to-protect-your-credit/

4. Frankel, R. S. and Tsosie, C. "7 Facts About 0% APR Credit Card Deals", NerdWallet, August 20, 2020.
Link: https://www.nerdwallet.com/article/credit-cards/facts-about-zero-percent-apr-credit-cards

5. Pritchard, J., "Escape the Debt Cycle", The Balance, November 29, 2020. Link: https://www.thebalance.com/get-out-of-the-debt-cycle-4054269